Vocabu-Lit

Reading Your Way to Word Power

H A W K

Table of Contents

Lesson 1. adapted from "The Monkey's Paw," W. W. Jacobs 1

Lesson 2. adapted from *Black Beauty*, Anna Sewell 5

Lesson 3. from a student 9

Lesson 4. adapted from *Through the Looking-Glass*, Lewis Carroll 13

Lesson 5. from *Twenty Thousand Leagues Under the Sea*, Jules Verne 17

Lesson 6. from *Durango Street*, Frank Bonham 21

Lesson 7. from "Why Banks Is Robbed in Texas," Henry Gregor Felsen 25

Lesson 8. from a student 29

Lesson 9. from *Cool Cat*, Frank Bonham . . . 33

Lesson 10. from *Kim*, Rudyard Kipling 37

Lesson 11. from *Five Little Peppers and How They Grew*, Margaret Sidney 41

Lesson 12. Review 45

Lesson 13. from *The Land of Oz*, L. Frank Baum 47

Lesson 14. from *Around the World in Eighty Days*, Jules Verne 51

Lesson 15. adapted from *Black Beauty*, Anna Sewell 55

Lesson 16. from *The Log of a Cowboy*, Andy Adams 59

Lesson 17. adapted from "The Happy Prince," Oscar Wilde 63

Lesson 18. from "First Jump," Henry Gregor Felsen 67

Lesson 19. from *Arabian Nights* 71

Lesson 20. from "The Revolt of Mother," Mary E. Wilkins Freeman 75

Lesson 21. adapted from *The Land of Oz*, L. Frank Baum 79

Lesson 22. from *Five Little Peppers and How They Grew*, Margaret Sidney 83

Lesson 23. from *Around the World in Eighty Days*, Jules Verne 87

Lesson 24. Review 91

Lesson 25. adapted from "A Little Cloud" from *Dubliners*, James Joyce 93

Lesson 26. from "Li Chang's Million," Henry Gregor Felsen 97

Lesson 27. from "The Happy Prince," Oscar Wilde 101

Lesson 28. adapted from *The Nitty Gritty*, Frank Bonham 105

Lesson 29. from *The Red Pony*, John Steinbeck 109

Lesson 30. from "The Legend of Sleepy Hollow," Washington Irving 113

Lesson 31. from *Five Little Peppers and How They Grew*, Margaret Sidney . . . 117

Lesson 32. from *The Old Man and the Sea*, Ernest Hemingway 121

Lesson 33. adapted from "The Luck of Roaring Camp," Bret Harte 125

Lesson 34. from *Walden*, Henry David Thoreau 129

Lesson 35. from "The Lady, or the Tiger?" Frank R. Stockton 133

Lesson 36. Review 137

Using the *Vocabu-Lit* Program

Vocabu-Lit is a unique lit-based program designed to help your students improve their word power. In format and approach, it differs in several ways from the usual vocabulary-building materials.

First, *Vocabu-Lit* contains examples of how the vocabulary words have been used by various writers and speakers. The inclusion of classic and high-interest literature not only will interest students in good writing but also will show them how vocabulary can become an effective writing tool.

Second, *Vocabu-Lit* does not ask students to learn a large number of words at one sitting. Instead, students master just ten words at a time and are provided several experiences with those words. Each experience reinforces the previous one, helping students to master meaning.

Third, *Vocabu-Lit* capitalizes on students' natural approach to language acquisition by having them study words in context. Learning words through context aids students in two ways. First, it leads them to define a word more precisely. It also helps them develop an important reading skill: the ability to discover and use contextual clues to determine meaning.

Reading the Passage

Each lesson begins with a selection from a book, essay, story, poem, or speech. Students are encouraged to read straight through the selection without paying particular attention to the Master Words (the ten words in dark type). Their understanding of the general meaning of the passage should help them determine the definitions of the Master Words. Students are advised to read the passage again, this time paying closer attention to the Master Words.

Self-testing for Understanding

The first exercise is a self-test designed to help students identify the words which they have not yet mastered. Often students will think they know a Master Word only to find that the contextual meaning of the word differs from their own understanding of its meaning. Or they may be unable to state the exact definition. This exercise teaches students to examine a word in context and define its meaning more precisely.

Sometimes the word is actually defined by the context. For example, "He was a *mendicant* because he had to beg." Other times, opposite or contrasting terms reveal the word's meaning: "He was far from poor; in fact, he was *affluent.*" Sometimes an unfamiliar word may be followed by examples which explain it, as in "Mrs. Murphy was a *hospitable* woman who warmly welcomed her son's friends." From the context, which in this case consists of an example, the students should have little difficulty figuring out that *hospitable* means "giving a friendly welcome to guests." Selections may also include key words such as *means, is, for example, in other words,* or *and so forth.* All of these are clues which help the students determine a word's meaning.

Note: In some cases, the form of the Master Word in the self-test is not the same as in the passage. Generally, these changes were made to provide students with a more commonly used form of the word.

Writing Definitions

In the second exercise, students are asked to write definitions of the Master Words. The first part of the exercise asks that they define as many of the ten words as they can without using a dictionary. Students should use contextual clues and any previous experience with the words to write their definitions.

The second part of the exercise asks that the students consult a dictionary and copy an appropriate definition for each word in the space provided. A reproducible glossary is provided in the back of this teacher's edition should you wish to substitute it for a dictionary.

Note: The part of speech of the words as they will be used in the *exercises* is already indicated in the exercise. This may be different from the words' function in the passage, but students may still find contextual clues helpful.

Choosing Synonyms and Antonyms

In this exercise, students pick a synonym and antonym for each Master Word. Before students begin the lesson, you may wish to review the meanings of *synonym* and *antonym.*

Since students may not be familiar with all

the words in the list of synonyms and antonyms, they may find it useful to keep dictionaries handy.

Note: There are no appropriate antonyms for some Master Words. In such cases, the antonym blank has been marked with an X. Also, a synonym or antonym may sometimes match more than one Master Word in the exercise. Both possible answers are indicated in the teacher edition.

Completing Analogies

In the fourth exercise, students complete word analogies using the Master Words. Again, students will be working with synonyms and antonyms (though different from those in the third exercise).

Before attempting to complete this activity, students should be shown how to read analogies. Try introducing them to the concept with the following example.

day   :night   ::rich   :_____

Tell students that the symbol **:** means "is to" and **::** means "as." Thus, the analogy could be read "Day is to night as rich is to _____."

Point out to students that the words *day* and *night* are opposites, or antonyms. So they should look for an antonym of *rich* in their list of Master Words. The Master Word *penniless* would be a correct response.

Fitting Words into Context

The next exercise includes ten sentences, which students complete with the appropriate Master Words. Each sentence supplies clues to help students select the best answer. Thus, while testing understanding of the new words, this exercise also provides another contextual setting for the Master Words.

Playing with the Words

In the final exercise, students use the Master Words to solve a variety of puzzles. Traditional games such as acrostics, crosswords, and word spirals are offered. But there are also more novel puzzles that challenge students to arrange words by degree, play associations, complete word fact tables, and invent definitions for portmanteau (or merged) Master Words. They are even invited to write stories using some of their newly acquired vocabulary.

Reviewing Knowledge

There are three review lessons in every *Vocabu-Lit* (Lessons 12, 24, and 36). Students test their mastery of the vocabulary words from the previous eleven lessons by completing sentences and analogies.

LESSON 1

Read the following selection to get the general meaning. Read it a second time, paying special attention to the words in dark type. Notice how they are used in sentences. These are Master Words. These are the words you will be working with in this lesson.

Adapted from **"The Monkey's Paw"**
by W. W. Jacobs

He took something out of his pocket and invited them to look at it. Mrs. White drew back in **disgust**, but her son, taking it, examined it **curiously**.

"And what is there special about it?" inquired Mr. White, as he took it from his son and, having examined it, placed it upon the table.

"It had a spell put on it by an old **fakir**," said the sergeant-major, "a very holy man. He wanted to show that **fate** ruled people's lives, and that those who **interfered** with fate did so to their sorrow. He put a spell on it so that three separate men could each have three wishes."

His manner was so **impressive** that his listeners were **conscious** that their light laughter **jarred** somewhat.

"Well, why don't you have three, sir?" said Herbert White cleverly.

The soldier regarded him in the way that middle age is likely to regard **presumptuous** youth. "I have," he said quietly, and his **blotchy** face whitened.

EXERCISE 1

SELF-TEST: After reading the above selection, do the following. Look at the Master Words below. Underline the words that you think you know. Circle the words that you are less sure about. Draw a square around the words you don't recognize.

MASTER WORDS

blotchy	**fate**
conscious	**impressive**
curious	**interfere**
disgust	**jar**
fakir	**presumptuous**

1

Read the selection on the preceding page again, this time paying special attention to the ten Master Words. In the (a) spaces provided below, write down what you think is the meaning of the word. After you have attempted a definition for each word, look up the word in a dictionary. In the (b) spaces, copy the appropriate dictionary definition.

1. **blotchy** (adj.)

   a. _____

   b. _____ covered with large irregular spots _____

2. **conscious** (adj.)

   a. _____

   b. _____ aware of what one is doing or what is going on _____

3. **curious** (adj.)

   a. _____

   b. _____ interested; eager to learn _____

4. **disgust** (n.)

   a. _____

   b. _____ a feeling of sickness or great dislike; obvious distaste _____

5. **fakir** (n.)

   a. _____

   b. _____ a Moslem or Hindu religious beggar, often one who claims to perform magic or miracles _____

6. **fate** (n.)

   a. _____

   b. _____ the force which supposedly determines what and how events occur before they occur _____

7. **impressive** (adj.)

   a. _____

   b. _____ producing awe and admiration _____

8. **interfere** (v.)

   a. _____

   b. _____ to meddle in other people's business; to come between _____

9. **jar** (v.)

   a. _____

   b. _____ to make a harsh, unpleasant sound; also, to have an irritating, grating effect _____

10. **presumptuous** (adj.)

   a. _____

   b. _____ rudely taking things for granted; overly bold and pushy _____

Use the following list of synonyms and antonyms to fill in the blanks. Some words have no antonyms. In such cases, the antonym blanks have been marked with an X.

aware	boring	distaste	grate	lull	shy
awesome	clear	enjoyment	indifferent	meddle	spotted
beggar	destiny	free will	interested	refrain	unconscious
bold					

	Synonyms	**Antonyms**
1. **disgust**	(distaste)	(enjoyment)
2. **curious**	(interested)	(indifferent)
3. **fakir**	(beggar)	X
4. **fate**	(destiny)	(free will)
5. **interfere**	(meddle)	(refrain)
6. **impressive**	(awesome)	(boring)
7. **conscious**	(aware)	(unconscious)
8. **jar**	(grate)	(lull)
9. **presumptuous**	(bold)	(shy)
10. **blotchy**	(spotted)	(clear)

Decide whether the first pair in the items below are synonyms or antonyms. Then choose the Master Word that shows a similar relation to the word(s) preceding the blank.

1. small	:little	::questioning	:	(curious)
2. tired	:weary	::pushy	:	(presumptuous)
3. thin	:slim	::blemished	:	(blotchy)
4. push	:pull	::ignore	:	(interfere)
5. night	:day	::pleasure	:	(disgust)
6. mistake	:error	::chance	:	(fate)
7. accept	:refuse	::soothe	:	(jar)
8. boss	:chief	::holy one	:	(fakir)
9. wet	:dry	::ordinary	:	(impressive)
10. soft	:hard	::unaware	:	(conscious)

3

The Master Words in this lesson are repeated below. From the Master Words, choose the appropriate word for the blank in each of the following sentences. Write the word in the numbered space provided at the right.

| blotchy | curious | fakir | impressive | jar |
| conscious | disgust | fate | interfere | presumptuous |

1. Ivan's skin became ...?... after eating the chestnuts, and he had to go to a doctor to clear up the rash.

1. __(blotchy)__

2. Powerful nations often ...?... in the affairs of smaller nations.

2. __(interfere)__

3. The burping contest that Mina found so amusing filled me with ...?... .

3. __(disgust)__

4. While raiding the cookie jar after school, the children were suddenly ...?... of their mother's angry stare.

4. __(conscious)__

5. (A, An) ...?... often lives a life of poverty and gets food by begging.

5. __(fakir)__

6. After working here only three weeks, Eva was ...?... enough to tell the boss how the office should be organized.

6. __(presumptuous)__

7. The football team had a very ...?... record of thirteen straight wins.

7. __(impressive)__

8. The peacock's harsh cries often ...?... the peaceful silence.

8. __(jar)__

9. Though I was ...?... about Zach's mysterious past, I knew it wasn't polite to pry.

9. __(curious)__

10. Many people blame ...?... for events which are really a result of their own actions.

10. __(fate)__

Fill in the chart below with the Master Word that fits each set of clues. Part of speech refers to the word's usage in the lesson. Use a dictionary when necessary.

Number of Syllables	Part of Speech	Other Clues	Master Word
3	adjective	what a dead cat might have been	1. __(curious)__
1	noun	literally means "what has been spoken"	2. __(fate)__
4	adjective	if you are rude, you are probably this	3. __(presumptuous)__
2	noun	Arabic origin	4. __(fakir)__
3	verb	"meddle" is its cousin	5. __(interfere)__
1	verb	not a container when used as a verb	6. __(jar)__
2	noun	reaction to a liar	7. __(disgust)__
3	adjective	a perfect record is this	8. __(impressive)__
2	adjective	one who is alert is this	9. __(conscious)__
2	adjective	"mottled" is a synonym	10. __(blotchy)__

LESSON 2

Read the following selection to get the general meaning. Read it a second time, paying special attention to the words in dark type. Notice how they are used in sentences. These are Master Words. These are the words you will be working with in this lesson.

Adapted from **Black Beauty**
by Anna Sewell

After Rory was **disabled** I often pulled the carriage with a mare named Peggy, who stood in the next stall to mine. She was a strong, well-made animal, of a bright **dun** color, beautifully **dappled**, and with a dark-brown mane and tail. There was no high **breeding** about her, but she was very pretty and **remarkably** sweet-tempered and willing. Still, there was an **anxious** look about her eye, by which I knew that she had some trouble. The first time we went out together I thought she had a very odd pace; she seemed to go partly in a trot, partly in a **canter**, three or four paces, and then to make a little jump forward.

It was very unpleasant for any horse who pulled with her, and made me quite **fidgety**.

When we got home I asked her what made her go in that odd, awkward way.

"Ah," she said in a troubled manner, "I know my paces are very bad, but what can I do? It really is not my fault; it is just because my legs are so short. I stand nearly as high as you, but your legs are a good three inches longer above your knees than mine, and of course you can take a much longer step and go much faster. You see I did not make myself. I wish I could have done so; I would have had long legs then. All my troubles come from my short legs," said Peggy, in a [**despondent**] tone.

"But how is it," I said, "when you are so strong and good-tempered and willing?"

"Why, you see," said she, "men will go so fast, and if one can't keep up to other horses it is nothing but whip, whip, whip, all the time. And so I have had to keep up as I could, and have got into this ugly **shuffling** pace. It was not always so; when I lived with my first master I always went a good regular trot, but then he was not in such a hurry . . . ."

EXERCISE 1

SELF-TEST: After reading the above selection, do the following. Look at the Master Words below. Underline the words that you think you know. Circle the words that you are less sure about. Draw a square around the words you don't recognize.

MASTER WORDS

anxious	disabled
breeding	dun
canter	fidgety
dappled	remarkable
despondent	shuffle

Read the selection on the preceding page again, this time paying special attention to the ten Master Words. In the (a) spaces provided below, write down what you think is the meaning of the word. After you have attempted a definition for each word, look up the word in a dictionary. In the (b) spaces, copy the appropriate dictionary definition.

1. **anxious** (adj.)

   a. _____

   b. ___ deeply concerned; troubled; worried; uneasy ___

2. **breeding** (n.)

   a. _____

   b. ___ upbringing and education; training in good behavior and manners ___

3. **canter** (n.)

   a. _____

   b. ___ a gait similar to an easy gallop ___

4. **dappled** (adj.)

   a. _____

   b. ___ marked with small spots ___

5. **despondent** (adj.)

   a. _____

   b. ___ depressed; without hope ___

6. **disabled** (adj.)

   a. _____

   b. ___ weakened; crippled; unable to function ___

7. **dun** (adj.)

   a. _____

   b. ___ dull brown or grayish-brown ___

8. **fidgety** (adj.)

   a. _____

   b. ___ uneasy; restless; moving nervously ___

9. **remarkable** (adj.)

   a. _____

   b. ___ worthy of notice; uncommon; wonderful; extraordinary ___

10. **shuffle** (v.)

   a. _____

   b. ___ to walk without lifting the feet or with an awkward gait ___

Use the following list of synonyms and antonyms to fill in the blanks. Some words have no antonyms. In such cases, the antonym blanks have been marked with an X.

cheerful   gallop   hopeless   prance   still   unusual
crippled   grayish-brown   jumpy   solid-colored   training   walk
crudeness   healed   ordinary   spotted   unconcerned   worried
drag

	Synonyms	**Antonyms**
1. **disabled**	(crippled)	(healed)
2. **dun**	(grayish-brown)	X
3. **dappled**	(spotted)	(solid-colored)
4. **breeding**	(training)	(crudeness)
5. **remarkable**	(unusual)	(ordinary)
6. **anxious**	(worried)	(unconcerned)
7. **canter**	(gallop)	(walk)
8. **fidgety**	(jumpy)	(still)
9. **despondent**	(hopeless)	(cheerful)
10. **shuffle**	(drag)	(prance) (gallop)

Decide whether the first pair in the items below are synonyms or antonyms. Then choose the Master Word that shows a similar relation to the word(s) preceding the blank.

1. fakir	:holy beggar	::run	:	(canter)
2. fate	:fortune	::speckled	:	(dappled)
3. disgust	:contentment	::relaxed	:	(anxious)
4. jar	:calm	::healthy	:	(disabled)
5. impressive	:average	::motionless	:	(fidgety)
6. conscious	:unknowing	::common	:	(remarkable)
7. interfere	:disregard	::happy	:	(despondent)
8. presumptuous	:sassy	::hobble	:	(shuffle)
9. curious	:intrigued	::upbringing	:	(breeding)
10. blotchy	:freckled	::drab	:	(dun)

The Master Words in this lesson are repeated below. From the Master Words, choose the appropriate word for the blank in each of the following sentences. Write the word in the numbered space provided at the right.

anxious   canter   despondent   dun   remarkable
breeding   dappled   disabled   fidgety   shuffle

1. Nicole was ...?... by the accident and could not work for several months until her leg healed.

1. _____ (disabled)

2. "You act like you just lost your best friend," Ethan remarked. "Why are you so ...?... ?"

2. _____ (despondent)

3. The tremendous amount of information children acquire in their first two years of life is truly ...?... .

3. _____ (remarkable)

4. From the air, we observed the ...?... pattern that the clouds made on the farmland.

4. _____ (dappled)

5. The wail of a tornado siren made the parents ...?... for the safety of their children, who had gone hiking in the woods.

5. _____ (anxious)

6. The ...?... child was bored and wanted to play outside.

6. _____ (fidgety)

7. The ...?... mule blended right into the brown canyon wall.

7. _____ (dun)

8. Our halfback, who had suffered an ankle injury in Friday night's game, ...?...(d, ed) into the auditorium.

8. _____ (shuffle)

9. Susan took her horse around the track at (a, an) ...?..., then slowed the animal to a walk.

9. _____ (canter)

10. Marvin, generous and polite, enjoyed classical music and the theater, but his brother showed no signs of ...?... whatsoever.

10. _____ (breeding)

To complete the word spiral, choose the Master Word associated with each phrase below. Start with 1 and fill in each answer clockwise. Be careful! Each new word may overlap the previous word by one or more letters.

1. easy pace for most horses

2. winning an Olympic medal, for example

3. more than just concerned

4. sliding or dragging step

5. pattern on a fawn's coat

6. mentally or physically weakened

7. khaki pants are this color

8. manners and education add up to this

9. another word for "antsy"

10. mood when you're ready to give up

1. C	A	N	T	E	2. R	E	M	A
A	P	P	L	E	6. D	I	S	R
5. D	G	9. F	I	D	G	E	A	K
E	N	D	E	N	T	T	B	A
L	I	N	■	■	■	Y	L	B
F	D	O	P	S	E	10. D	E	L
F	E	E	R	8. B	N	U	7. D	E
U	H	4. S	U	O	I	X	N	3. A

LESSON 3

Read the following selection to get the general meaning. Read it a second time, paying special attention to the words in dark type. Notice how they are used in sentences. These are Master Words. These are the words you will be working with in this lesson.

One of the major duties of a candy-striper is to **distribute** the hospital trays at mealtimes. Once I was told to feed an old man who was unable to feed himself. At first I was unwilling to perform this task, but I finally agreed to do so.

The old man looked up as I entered his room. He must have been very old, for his loose gray skin hung in folds and **pouches** all over his arms and head. What hair he had left was very thin and white. As I approached with his tray, he followed me with his eyes but didn't speak. In fact, he never spoke.

The small bites of food I offered were accepted and soon disappeared in the small toothless mouth. **Aside** from the **mechanical** chewing,

he made no movement at all. My **sympathy** went out to him, a poor old man with few years to live, if, indeed, he had any.

He seemed to take forever to finish his meal, for he **relished** every bite as if it were his very first, or last. His milky brown eyes, dull with age, stared at me **constantly** as I gave him the food.

When he finally finished, I **murmured** something polite and started to leave. As I reached the door, I **hesitated** and glanced back at him, a dying soul in an **antiseptic** prison. Although I can't be sure, I felt that underneath all his wrinkles he was smiling at me.

—Student

EXERCISE 1

SELF-TEST: After reading the above selection, do the following. Look at the Master Words below. Underline the words that you think you know. Circle the words that you are less sure about. Draw a square around the words you don't recognize.

MASTER WORDS

antiseptic	mechanical
aside	murmur
constant	pouch
distribute	relish
hesitate	sympathy

Read the selection on the preceding page again, this time paying special attention to the ten Master Words. In the (a) spaces provided below, write down what you think is the meaning of the word. After you have attempted a definition for each word, look up the word in a dictionary. In the (b) spaces, copy the appropriate dictionary definition.

1. **antiseptic** (adj.)

   a. _____

   b. _____ thoroughly clean _____

2. **aside** (adv.)

   a. _____

   b. _____ apart (from); except (for); excluding ____

3. **constant** (adj.)

   a. _____

   b. _____ continuing without a break _____

4. **distribute** (v.)

   a. _____

   b. _____ to divide among several or many; to deal out ____

5. **hesitate** (v.)

   a. _____

   b. _____ to pause briefly, perhaps due to doubt or indecision ____

6. **mechanical** (adj.)

   a. _____

   b. _____ performed as if by a machine or from habit ____

7. **murmur** (v.)

   a. _____

   b. _____ to make a low, indistinct sound ____

8. **pouch** (n.)

   a. _____

   b. _____ a bag or a sack ____

9. **relish** (v.)

   a. _____

   b. _____ to take pleasure in, especially to eat or drink with pleasure ____

10. **sympathy** (n.)

   a. _____

   b. _____ the act of entering into and sharing the feelings of another person, especially pity ____

Use the following list of synonyms and antonyms to fill in the blanks. Some words have no antonyms. In such cases, the antonym blanks have been marked with an X.

apart	conscious	deliver	enjoy	hardheartedness	pause
automatic	continual	dirty	gather	including	shout
bag	continue	dislike	germ-free	occasional	whisper
concern					

	Synonyms	**Antonyms**
1. **distribute**	(deliver)	(gather)
2. **pouch**	(bag)	X
3. **aside**	(apart)	(including)
4. **mechanical**	(automatic)	(conscious)
5. **sympathy**	(concern)	(hardheartedness)
6. **relish**	(enjoy)	(dislike)
7. **constant**	(continual)	(occasional)
8. **murmur**	(whisper)	(shout)
9. **hesitate**	(pause)	(continue)
10. **antiseptic**	(germ-free)	(dirty)

Decide whether the first pair in the items below are synonyms or antonyms. Then choose the Master Word that shows a similar relation to the word(s) preceding the blank.

1. canter	:jog	::wait	: (hesitate)
2. anxious	:calm	::yell	: (murmur)
3. disabled	:able-bodied	::hate	: (relish)
4. dappled	:blotchy	::robotlike	: (mechanical)
5. fidgety	:relaxed	::collect	: (distribute)
6. despondent	:merry	::mockery	: (sympathy)
7. breeding	:education	::sack	: (pouch)
8. remarkable	:average	::irregular	: (constant)
9. dun	:muddy	::sterile	: (antiseptic)
10. shuffle	:drag	::except	: (aside)

The Master Words in this lesson are repeated below. From the Master Words, choose the appropriate word for the blank in each of the following sentences. Write the word in the numbered space provided at the right.

antiseptic	constant	hesitate	murmur	relish
aside	distribute	mechanical	pouch	sympathy

1. ...?... from the tax issue, I found myself in agreement with the candidate's major policies.

1. _____ (aside)

2. In an operating room everything must be ...?... so that a patient will not catch a disease.

2. _____ (antiseptic)

3. Correct use of a ZIP code helps postal workers to ...?... the mail.

3. _____ (distribute)

4. A baby kangaroo, about the size of a bee when it is born, spends four to five months in its mother's ...?... .

4. _____ (pouch)

5. Mother's answer was ...?...; she hadn't listened to my question.

5. _____ (mechanical)

6. I was standing close enough to hear Regina ...?... a reply.

6. _____ (murmur)

7. The quarterback ...?...(d, ed) for a long moment before finally passing the ball to Lance.

7. _____ (hesitate)

8. A ...?..., driving rain resulted in flood waters which spilled into the Nishna Valley.

8. _____ (constant)

9. The ...?... of my friends helped me get over the disappointment of not winning the contest.

9. _____ (sympathy)

10. Students often ...?... the thought of vacation, only to find that they haven't enough activities to fill their leisure hours.

10. _____ (relish)

To complete this puzzle, fill in the Master Word associated with each phrase below. Then unscramble the circled letters to form a Master Word from Lesson 2, and define it.

1. to pause in doubt

h (e) s i t a t e

2. what postal carriers do with the mail

(d) i s (t) r i b u t e

3. apart from that

a s i (d) e

4. cleaner than clean

a n t i s e p t i c

5. you might feel this for a friend who is ill

s y m (p) a t h y

6. all the time

c o n s t (a) n t

7. soft sound

m u r m u r

8. lick your lips

r e (l) i s h

9. like a puppet's movements

m e c h a n i c a l

10. this can be a purse or a knapsack

(p) o u c h

Unscrambled word: _____ (dappled)

Definition: _____ (marked with small spots)

(Note: Definition may vary.)

Read the following selection to get the general meaning. Read it a second time, paying special attention to the words in dark type. Notice how they are used in sentences. These are Master Words. These are the words you will be working with in this lesson.

Adapted from **Through the Looking Glass** by Lewis Carroll

"I see nobody on the road," said Alice.

"I only wish *I* had such eyes," the King remarked in a **fretful** tone. "To be able to see Nobody! And at that distance too! Why, it's as much as *I* can do to see real people, by this light!"

All this was lost on Alice, who was still looking **intently** along the road, shading her eyes with one hand. "I see somebody now!" she exclaimed at last. "But he's coming very slowly — and what curious **attitudes** he goes into!" (For the Messenger kept skipping up and down, and **wriggling** like an eel, as he came along, with his great hands spread out like fans on each side.)

The Messenger, to Alice's great amusement, opened a bag that hung round his neck, and handed a sandwich to the King, who **devoured** it **greedily**.

"Another sandwich!" said the King.

"There's nothing but hay left now," the Messenger said, peeping into the bag.

"Hay, then," the king murmured in a faint whisper.

Alice was glad to see that it [**refreshed**] him a good deal. "There's nothing like eating hay when you're faint," he remarked to her, as he **munched** away.

"I should think throwing cold water over you would be better," Alice suggested.

"I didn't say there was nothing *better*," the King replied. "I said there was nothing *like* it." Which Alice did not **venture** to **deny**.

EXERCISE 1

SELF-TEST: After reading the above selection, do the following. Look at the Master Words below. Underline the words that you think you know. Circle the words that you are less sure about. Draw a square around the words you don't recognize.

MASTER WORDS

attitude	intent
deny	munch
devour	refresh
fretful	venture
greedily	wriggle

Read the selection on the preceding page again, this time paying special attention to the ten Master Words. In the (a) spaces provided below, write down what you think is the meaning of the word. After you have attempted a definition for each word, look up the word in a dictionary. In the (b) spaces, copy the appropriate dictionary definition.

1. **attitude** (n.)

   a. _____

   b. _____ posture; physical position of the body _____

2. **deny** (v.)

   a. _____

   b. _____ to declare that something is untrue _____

3. **devour** (v.)

   a. _____

   b. _____ to eat quickly and hungrily _____

4. **fretful** (adj.)

   a. _____

   b. _____ irritable; worried; discontented; impatient _____

5. **greedily** (adv.)

   a. _____

   b. _____ eagerly; ravenously _____

6. **intent** (adj.)

   a. _____

   b. _____ directed with eager or fixed attention _____

7. **munch** (v.)

   a. _____

   b. _____ to chew steadily or vigorously, often with a crunching sound _____

8. **refresh** (v.)

   a. _____

   b. _____ to restore strength or spirit to; to revive or put new life into _____

9. **venture** (v.)

   a. _____

   b. _____ to dare to say at the risk of criticism, argument, etc. _____

10. **wriggle** (v.)

   a. _____

   b. _____ to twist to and fro; to squirm _____

EXERCISE 3

Use the following list of synonyms and antonyms to fill in the blanks. Some words have no antonyms. In such cases, the antonym blanks have been marked with an X.

absent-minded	chew	disclaim	irritable	relaxed
absorbed	consume	exhaust	politely	renew
admit	dare	hungrily	position	squirm
avoid				

		Synonyms	**Antonyms**
1.	**fretful**	(irritable)	(relaxed)
2.	**intent**	(absorbed)	(absent-minded)
3.	**attitude**	(position)	X
4.	**wriggle**	(squirm)	X
5.	**devour**	(consume)	X
6.	**greedily**	(hungrily)	(politely)
7.	**refresh**	(renew)	(exhaust)
8.	**munch**	(chew)	X
9.	**venture**	(dare)	(avoid)
10.	**deny**	(disclaim)	(admit)

EXERCISE 4

Decide whether the first pair in the items below are synonyms or antonyms. Then choose the Master Word that shows a similar relation to the word(s) preceding the blank.

1.	murmur	:scream	::agree with	:	(deny)
2.	hesitate	:delay	::nibble	:	(munch)
3.	mechanical	:unconscious	::pose	:	(attitude)
4.	relish	:delight in	::interested	:	(intent)
5.	pouch	:purse	::gobble	:	(devour)
6.	distribute	:circulate	::selfishly	:	(greedily)
7.	sympathy	:indifference	::tire	:	(refresh)
8.	antiseptic	:disinfected	::twist	:	(wriggle)
9.	aside	:besides	::attempt	:	(venture)
10.	constant	:now and then	::calm	:	(fretful)

The Master Words in this lesson are repeated below. From the Master Words, choose the appropriate word for the blank in each of the following sentences. Write the word in the numbered space provided at the right.

attitude	devour	greedily	munch	venture
deny	fretful	intent	refresh	wriggle

1. The travelers ...?...(d, ed) themselves at the cool well before continuing their journey through the desert.

1. _____ (refresh)

2. The reckless ...?... of the man on the tightrope made the audience laugh and gasp.

2. _____ (attitude)

3. It doesn't bother me when my roommate quietly eats his yogurt, but I can't study when he begins to ...?... on potato chips.

3. _____ (munch)

4. All of us were too embarrassed to ask except for Meg, who ...?...(d, ed) the question without a blush.

4. _____ (venture)

5. When a ten-foot snake uncoils, its tail soon begins to ...?... .

5. _____ (wriggle)

6. The selfish little boy ...?... ate the pizza without offering his friends a bite.

6. _____ (greedily)

7. The suspect did not ...?... that he had been in the store on the night of the crime, but he did swear he was not the robber.

7. _____ (deny)

8. Robert was able to ...?... three gallons of ice cream in fourteen minutes during the Fourth of July celebration.

8. _____ (devour)

9. When one person in a family is short-tempered, others, too, may soon become ...?... .

9. _____ (fretful)

10. Shelley was ...?... upon her sewing as she hurried to finish her new shirt for the party.

10. _____ (intent)

To complete the crossword, choose the Master Word associated with each word or phrase below. Begin each answer in the square having the same number as the clue.

1. cold lemonade will do this on a hot day

2. "chow down"

3. move like a worm on a hook

4. you might eat this way after a day without food

5. you do this when you eat popcorn

6. to take a chance

7. uneasy and restless

8. someone focused on a task is this

9. "I did not!"

10. body position

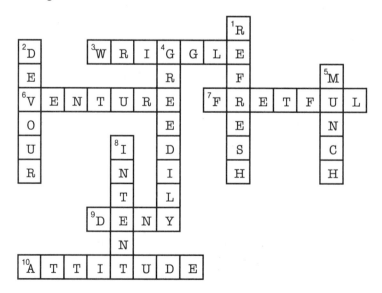

Read the following selection to get the general meaning. Read it a second time, paying special attention to the words in dark type. Notice how they are used in sentences. These are Master Words. These are the words you will be working with in this lesson.

From **Twenty Thousand Leagues Under the Sea** by Jules Verne

. . . Everything was frozen—even the noise. The *Nautilus* was then **obliged** to stop in its **adventurous** course amid these fields of ice. In spite of our efforts, in spite of the powerful means **employed** to break up the ice, the *Nautilus* remained **immovable**. Generally, when we can proceed no further, we have return still open to us; but here return was as impossible as advance, for every pass had closed behind us; . . . I was obliged to admit that Captain Nemo was more than **imprudent**. I was on the platform at that moment. The Captain had been observing our situation for some time past, when he said to me—

"Well, sir, what do you think of this?"

"I think that we are caught, Captain."

"So, M. Aronnax, you really think that the *Nautilus* cannot **disengage** itself?"

"With difficulty, Captain; for the season is already too far advanced for you to [**rely**] on the breaking up of the ice."

"Ah! sir," said Captain Nemo, in an **ironical** tone, "you will always be the same. You see nothing but difficulties and **obstacles**. I **affirm** that not only can the *Nautilus* disengage itself, but also that it can go further still."

"Further to the south?" I asked, looking at the Captain.

"Yes, sir; it shall go to the pole."

EXERCISE 1

SELF-TEST: After reading the above selection, do the following. Look at the Master Words below. Underline the words that you think you know. Circle the words that you are less sure about. Draw a square around the words you don't recognize.

MASTER WORDS

adventurous	**imprudent**
affirm	**ironical**
disengage	**oblige**
employ	**obstacle**
immovable	**rely**

Read the selection on the preceding page again, this time paying special attention to the ten Master Words. In the (a) spaces provided below, write down what you think is the meaning of the word. After you have attempted a definition for each word, look up the word in a dictionary. In the (b) spaces, copy the appropriate dictionary definition.

1. **adventurous** (adj.)

   a. _____

   b. _____ involving a risk; courageous _____

2. **affirm** (v.)

   a. _____

   b. _____ to declare something to be true or factual _____

3. **disengage** (v.)

   a. _____

   b. _____ to release or detach; to set free _____

4. **employ** (v.)

   a. _____

   b. _____ to make use of _____

5. **immovable** (adj.)

   a. _____

   b. _____ incapable of being moved; fixed; stationary; motionless _____

6. **imprudent** (adj.)

   a. _____

   b. _____ lacking caution and good judgment; rash; unwise _____

7. **ironical** (adj.)

   a. _____

   b. _____ mocking or sarcastic; implying the opposite of what is said or written _____

8. **oblige** (v.)

   a. _____

   b. _____ to force as a result of circumstances; to bind or obligate _____

9. **obstacle** (n.)

   a. _____

   b. _____ that which stands in the way; a barrier _____

10. **rely** (v.)

    a. _____

    b. _____ to count on; to depend on; also, to trust _____

Use the following list of synonyms and antonyms to fill in the blanks. Some words have no antonyms. In such cases, the antonym blanks have been marked with an X.

aid	deny	movable	require	sincere	unwise
barrier	depend	permit	satirical	stuck	use
bind	discard	release	sensible	timid	vow
daring	distrust				

	Synonyms	**Antonyms**
1. **oblige**	(require)	(permit) (release)
2. **adventurous**	(daring)	(timid)
3. **employ**	(use)	(discard)
4. **immovable**	(stuck)	(movable)
5. **imprudent**	(unwise)	(sensible)
6. **disengage**	(release)	(bind)
7. **rely**	(depend)	(distrust)
8. **ironical**	(satirical)	(sincere)
9. **obstacle**	(barrier)	(aid)
10. **affirm**	(vow)	(deny)

Decide whether the first pair in the items below are synonyms or antonyms. Then choose the Master Word that shows a similar relation to the word(s) preceding the blank.

1. munch	:gnaw	::loosen	:	(disengage)
2. attitude	:posture	::try out	:	(employ)
3. devour	:gulp	::trust	:	(rely)
4. deny	:reject	::force	:	(oblige)
5. intent	:bored	::portable	:	(immovable)
6. wriggle	:wiggle	::hurdle	:	(obstacle)
7. greedily	:moderately	::wise	:	(imprudent)
8. venture	:try	::bold	:	(adventurous)
9. refresh	:weary	::doubt	:	(affirm)
10. fretful	:peaceful	::serious	:	(ironical)

The Master Words in this lesson are repeated below. From the Master Words, choose the appropriate word for the blank in each of the following sentences. Write the word in the numbered space provided at the right.

adventurous	disengage	immovable	ironical	obstacle
affirm	employ	imprudent	oblige	rely

1. The hurdler cleared every ...?... on the track and won the race.

1. _(obstacle)_

2. The voyages to the moon were exciting and ...?... missions.

2. _(adventurous)_

3. Although the worried parents ...?...(d, ed) all means available to them, they could find no trace of their missing daughter.

3. _(employ)_

4. The candidate could ...?... on the support of only 932 delegates; it would be an open convention.

4. _(rely)_

5. Union leaders remained ...?... in their demand for higher wages no matter what management said.

5. _(immovable)_

6. We realized we would have to call a wrecker to ...?... the two locked bumpers.

6. _(disengage)_

7. You must learn to determine when speakers or writers are being ...?... and when they are being straightforward.

7. _(ironical)_

8. Because the bridge was gone, the men were ...?...(d, ed) to find another way across the river.

8. _(oblige)_

9. Though no one believed the poor woman, she ...?...(d, ed) over and over that she was once wealthy.

9. _(affirm)_

10. Riding a bicycle at night without adequate lights and reflectors is nothing short of ...?... .

10. _(imprudent)_

Write the Master Word that is associated with each word group below. Then list three things that might be associated with the review word that follows.

1. steeplechase, problem, roadblock — _(obstacle)_

2. unbolt, disconnect, free — _(disengage)_

3. operate, practice, handle — _(employ)_

4. drunk driving, gambling, stealing — _(imprudent)_

5. skydiving, bullfighting, mountain climbing — _(adventurous)_

6. North Star, Old Faithful, Rock of Gibraltar — _(immovable)_

7. pledges, beliefs, sermons — _(affirm)_

8. contracts, treaties, promises — _(oblige)_

9. satire, jabs, puns — _(ironical)_

10. gravity, friends, alarm clocks — _(rely)_

Review word: shuffle (Lesson 2)

(feet) _(cards)_ _(papers)_

(Note: Answers may vary.)

LESSON 6

Read the following selection to get the general meaning. Read it a second time, paying special attention to the words in dark type. Notice how they are used in sentences. These are Master Words. These are the words you will be working with in this lesson.

From **Durango Street**
by Frank Bonham

Mr. Rubio **chuckled** and blew a speck of paper from his desk **blotter**. "I hear you're a crew leader now," he said. "How do you like the job?"

Rufus grinned. "Fine. When I say 'frog,' those cats better jump."

Mr. Rubio wiggled a pencil **reflectively**. "What if a cat didn't jump?" he asked. "What would you do?"

Rufus smelled another of the sly **gambits** with which he was always trying to get him to explain why he had stolen and wrecked that automobile and got himself shipped to Pine Valley. But inside Rufus's mind was one place they were not going—not today, not tomorrow, not next year. So he merely **shrugged** and looked out the window again.

The social worker wrote something on a paper in Rufus's folder. "You haven't had many letters from your mother since you came here, it seems to me," he said thoughtfully.

"No. My old lady would rather lose a tooth than write a letter."

"Lots of people hate to write letters. I'm glad you understand that, and that your feelings aren't hurt."

Something about the statement **irritated** Rufus. He **gazed** unblinking across the desk.

"Why should my feelings be hurt?" he said. "That's stupid, letting anybody get at you that way. I've got twenty kids in my crew, and some cat's always giving me a hard time—trying to make a fool of me in front of the gang. But ol' Rufus stays on top of things. Let somebody else get his feelings hurt—I got too much to do."

Mr. Rubio nodded seriously. "Excellent **philosophy**," he said. "In fact—" Then he hesitated. Rufus **suspected** that he wanted to move quickly to another subject, but felt he must do it smoothly. He wiggled his pencil again and finally said:

"In a way, that ability to stay on top of things is the difference between a bench warmer and a first-string halfback. Wouldn't you say?"

In Rufus's mind a red light flashed beside the tracks. Last week, too, Mr. Rubio had mentioned football. And both times he had talked about halfbacks!

Now, that was more than **coincidence**.

"I guess you're right," he said calmly.

—Durango Street *by Frank Bonham. Copyright 1965 by Frank Bonham. E. P. Dutton and Co., Publishers.*

EXERCISE 1

SELF-TEST: After reading the above selection, do the following. Look at the Master Words below. Underline the words that you think you know. Circle the words that you are less sure about. Draw a square around the words you don't recognize.

MASTER WORDS

blotter	**gaze**	**reflective**
chuckle	**irritate**	**shrug**
coincidence	**philosophy**	**suspect**
gambit		

Read the selection on the preceding page again, this time paying special attention to the ten Master Words. In the (a) spaces provided below, write down what you think is the meaning of the word. After you have attempted a definition for each word, look up the word in a dictionary. In the (b) spaces, copy the appropriate dictionary definition.

1. **blotter** (n.)

    a. _____

    b. ___paper used for absorbing excess ink_____

2. **chuckle** (v.)

    a. _____

    b. ___to laugh quietly to oneself, often with the feeling of satisfaction___

3. **coincidence** (n.)

    a. _____

    b. ___an unusual occurrence of two or more events at one time, apparently by chance___

4. **gambit** (n.)

    a. _____

    b. ___a maneuver by which one intends to gain an advantage over an opponent___

5. **gaze** (v.)

    a. _____

    b. ___to look at steadily or intently_____

6. **irritate** (v.)

    a. _____

    b. ___to cause one to be impatient, angry, or displeased; to bother or annoy___

7. **philosophy** (n.)

    a. _____

    b. ___a system of principles for guidance in daily living___

8. **reflective** (adj.)

    a. _____

    b. ___thoughtful; pondering; meditative_____

9. **shrug** (v.)

    a. _____

    b. ___to raise and lower the shoulders, often expressing uncertainty or indifference___

10. **suspect** (v.)

    a. _____

    b. ___to imagine something to be true or likely_____

Use the following list of synonyms and antonyms to fill in the blanks. Some words have no antonyms. In such cases, the antonym blanks have been marked with an X.

chance	know	pad	shake	tactic
cry	laugh	peek	soothe	thoughtful
disturb	outlook	plan	stare	unthinking
guess				

	Synonyms	**Antonyms**
1. **chuckle**	(laugh)	(cry)
2. **blotter**	(pad)	X
3. **reflective**	(thoughtful)	(unthinking)
4. **gambit**	(tactic)	X
5. **shrug**	(shake)	X
6. **irritate**	(disturb)	(soothe)
7. **gaze**	(stare)	(peek)
8. **philosophy**	(outlook)	X
9. **suspect**	(guess)	(know)
10. **coincidence**	(chance)	(plan)

Decide whether the first pair in the items below are synonyms or antonyms. Then choose the Master Word that shows a similar relation to the word(s) preceding the blank.

1. oblige	:excuse	::design	:	(coincidence)
2. immovable	:mobile	::impulsive	:	(reflective)
3. disengage	:untie	::look at	:	(gaze)
4. employ	:utilize	::strategy	:	(gambit)
5. imprudent	:practical	::weep	:	(chuckle)
6. rely	:count on	::raise and lower	:	(shrug)
7. affirm	:declare	::suppose	:	(suspect)
8. obstacle	:roadblock	::absorbent paper	:	(blotter)
9. adventurous	:heroic	::viewpoint	:	(philosophy)
10. ironical	:straightforward	::please	:	(irritate)

The Master Words in this lesson are repeated below. From the Master Words, choose the appropriate word for the blank in each of the following sentences. Write the word in the numbered space provided at the right.

| blotter | coincidence | gaze | philosophy | shrug |
| chuckle | gambit | irritate | reflective | suspect |

1. The ...?... Julian lived by was to take one day at a time.

1. _____ (philosophy)

2. The principal became angry when the pupil continued to ...?... in response to his questions.

2. _____ (shrug)

3. That I had $4.05 in my wallet—the exact cost of my purchase— was a lucky ...?... .

3. _____ (coincidence)

4. A secondary function of (a, an) ...?... is to protect the surface of a desk from being scratched.

4. _____ (blotter)

5. Grandma opened the chess game with a bold ...?..., and John could feel himself on the defensive already.

5. _____ (gambit)

6. Although he ...?...(d, ed) after the speeding car, the policeman was unable to read the license number.

6. _____ (gaze)

7. I have no proof, but I ...?... Ken broke my car window.

7. _____ (suspect)

8. The puppy's amusing tricks made us all smile and ...?... .

8. _____ (chuckle)

9. Mary continued to practice her piano lesson; the repetition of so few notes began to ...?... everyone in the room.

9. _____ (irritate)

10. Whenever I finish a book, I spend a few ...?... moments relating what I read to my own life.

10. _____ (reflective)

Fill in the chart below with the Master Word that fits each set of clues. Part of speech refers to the word's usage in the lesson. Use a dictionary when necessary.

Number of Syllables	Part of Speech	Other Clues	Master Word
2	noun	also a chess move	1. _____ (gambit)
3	adjective	in a thinking mood	2. _____ (reflective)
2	verb	you do this when tickled	3. _____ (chuckle)
3	verb	delays or insults may do this	4. _____ (irritate)
1	verb	this gesture may mean "I don't know"	5. _____ (shrug)
2	noun	it soaks up ink	6. _____ (blotter)
4	noun	Greek root means "loving"	7. _____ (philosophy)
2	verb	what a Doubting Thomas does	8. _____ (suspect)
1	verb	you might do this on starry nights	9. _____ (gaze)
4	noun	being born and dying on the same day is an example	10. _____ (coincidence)

Read the following selection to get the general meaning. Read it a second time, paying special attention to the words in dark type. Notice how they are used in sentences. These are Master Words. These are the words you will be working with in this lesson.

From **"Why Banks Is Robbed in Texas"**
by Henry Gregor Felsen

In Texas, Curly Kid was used to riding the open plains until he came to a place where there was a little string of saloons and stores on one side of the trail, and another little string of saloons and stores on the other, and that was town. And the only difference between the big towns and the little towns, was that the big towns [were] somewhat longer than the little towns. And he was **expert** at riding into one end of a town, robbing the bank, shooting anybody that moved, and riding out the other end with a **posse** hot on his heels. And, naturally, he had **assumed** that he would follow this proven method of robbery in Oklahoma City—the moment he discovered which side of the street the bank was on.

But . . . ! Instead of following the natural, rightful Texas **pattern**, [those] dumb Oklahomans had built a dozen or more streets all running side by side in the same direction; which was about the silliest **duplication** of effort Curly Kid had ever seen. And, to make matters worse, they had allowed a whole mess of streets to spring up that **intersected** with these first streets.

As a result of this lack of planning, there was a big **junction** every hundred yards or so, jammed with people and horses and wagons and cattle, all trying to cross the same piece of ground, in different directions, and at the same time. Naturally, it couldn't be done.

It was a **marvel** to Curly Kid how people living so close to Texas could have such strange ways, and he could have watched for hours, chuckling and **exclaiming** to himself over the **antics** of [those] crazy Oklahomans. But he had business to attend to, and he was too serious about his work to let entertainment interfere with it for more than a minute.

—"Why Banks Is Robbed in Texas" by Henry Gregor Felsen. Copyright 1968 by Henry Gregor Felsen.

EXERCISE 1

SELF-TEST: After reading the above selection, do the following. Look at the Master Words below. Underline the words that you think you know. Circle the words that you are less sure about. Draw a square around the words you don't recognize.

MASTER WORDS

antics	**intersect**
assume	**junction**
duplication	**marvel**
exclaim	**pattern**
expert	**posse**

Read the selection on the preceding page again, this time paying special attention to the ten Master Words. In the (a) spaces provided below, write down what you think is the meaning of the word. After you have attempted a definition for each word, look up the word in a dictionary. In the (b) spaces, copy the appropriate dictionary definition.

1. **antics** (n.)

   a. _____

   b. ___ humorous, strange, or fantastic gestures, positions, or tricks ___

2. **assume** (v.)

   a. _____

   b. ___ to take for granted; to suppose ___

3. **duplication** (n.)

   a. _____

   b. ___ a thing identical to something else; a replica or copy ___

4. **exclaim** (v.)

   a. _____

   b. ___ to cry out or speak loudly, as from surprise or strong emotion ___

5. **expert** (adj.)

   a. _____

   b. ___ having special skill, knowledge, or training ___

6. **intersect** (v.)

   a. _____

   b. ___ to meet or join by passing through or across ___

7. **junction** (n.)

   a. _____

   b. ___ a place where things, such as railroads, streets, or rivers, come together ___

8. **marvel** (n.)

   a. _____

   b. ___ something which causes wonder or amazement ___

9. **pattern** (n.)

   a. _____

   b. ___ a design or arrangement; also, a model or guide ___

10. **posse** (n.)

   a. _____

   b. ___ a group of persons with legal power to help a sheriff keep the peace ___

Use the following list of synonyms and antonyms to fill in the blanks. Some words have no antonyms. In such cases, the antonym blanks have been marked with an X.

amateurish	crossroads	know	outlaws	shout	tricks
commonplace	design	lawmen	parallel	skillful	whisper
copy	disorder	original	separation	suppose	wonder
cross					

		Synonyms	**Antonyms**
1. **expert**	(skillful)	(amateurish)
2. **posse**	(lawmen)	(outlaws)
3. **assume**	(suppose)	(know)
4. **pattern**	(design)	(disorder)
5. **duplication**	(copy)	(original)
6. **intersect**	(cross)	(parallel)
7. **junction**	(crossroads) (cross)	(separation)
8. **marvel**	(wonder)	(commonplace)
9. **exclaim**	(shout)	(whisper)
10. **antics**	(tricks)	X

Decide whether the first pair in the items below are synonyms or antonyms. Then choose the Master Word that shows a similar relation to the word(s) preceding the blank.

1. gaze	:watch	::believe	: (assume)
2. gambit	:move	::foolishness	: (antics)
3. coincidence	:scheme	::murmur	: (exclaim)
4. shrug	:toss	::outline	: (pattern)
5. reflective	:concentrating	::amazement	: (marvel)
6. blotter	:pad	::crossing	: (junction)
7. philosophy	:beliefs	::connect	: (intersect)
8. chuckle	:sob	::unskilled	: (expert)
9. suspect	:confirm	::one-of-a-kind	: (duplication)
10. irritate	:calm	::criminals	: (posse)

The Master Words in this lesson are repeated below. From the Master Words, choose the appropriate word for the blank in each of the following sentences. Write the word in the numbered space provided at the right.

antics	duplication	expert	junction	pattern
assume	exclaim	intersect	marvel	posse

1. Thousands of tourists come to the Grand Canyon each year to gaze and wonder at one of nature's greatest ...?...(s).

1. _____ (marvel) _____

2. Major cities often spring up at the ...?... of two rivers.

2. _____ (junction) _____

3. The ...?... of the clown as he pranced around the ring were a delight to young and old alike.

3. _____ (antics) _____

4. Photocopying machines have made the ...?... of important papers a simple matter.

4. _____ (duplication) _____

5. Only the most ...?... mathematicians could solve the difficult problem.

5. _____ (expert) _____

6. Members of the drill team marched across the field in two lines which would ...?... at midfield.

6. _____ (intersect) _____

7. Oriental rugs are known for their fine workmanship and detailed ...?...(s).

7. _____ (pattern) _____

8. I ...?... Paul and Sue will be married soon after their engagement.

8. _____ (assume) _____

9. The sheriff rounded up (a, an) ...?... to help him track the bank robbers.

9. _____ (posse) _____

10. As Paul Revere rode through New England towns, he ...?...(d, ed), "The British are coming!"

10. _____ (exclaim) _____

Use at least five Master Words from this lesson to write a scene about one of the following topics. Or create a topic of your own. Write your choice on the blank. Circle the Master Words as you use them.

Possible Topics: Wandering Through a Foreign City, Incident at the Crossroads

_____

_____

_____

_____

_____

_____

_____

(Note: Answers will vary.)

LESSON 8

Read the following selection to get the general meaning. Read it a second time, paying special attention to the words in dark type. Notice how they are used in sentences. These are Master Words. These are the words you will be working with in this lesson.

The sign in the restaurant window read, "All Help Needed." John's spirits rose and the **despair** he had felt for months suddenly lifted. He opened the door of the restaurant and was greeted by the smiling face of the **maitre d'**. "Table, sir?"

John was so anxious that his words ran together. "Sir, I saw the sign, you know, I need a job and wondered if I could speak to the manager . . ."

The maitre d' looked more closely at John and his smile disappeared. "Yes, well, come along, then. I'm not certain that there are any jobs left."

"But I saw a sign."

"Yes, but it's been up for weeks and there have been many **applicants**. The manager should have taken the sign down days ago."

John was still hopeful as the maitre d' led him down a long hallway toward the manager's office. The manager would be the one to do the hiring.

The maitre d' knocked on the manager's door. "Come in," barked a voice. The maitre d' opened the door and John followed him into the room.

The manager sat **tilted** back in his chair with his shoes **propped** upon his otherwise bare desk. He was a tall, thin man with a hooked nose and arched brows over eyes that stared at John with **suspicion**.

"Mr. Jenson, this boy is looking for a job. I told him that there have been many applicants, and that it was **entirely** my fault the sign was still up."

The manager closed the magazine he was reading, leaving his bony forefinger between the pages to keep his place. The maitre d' left, closing the door gently behind him.

"I'm afraid he's right, son. I'm sorry that the sign was still up and **misled** you. Do you want to write down your name and address?"

Dutifully, John wrote out his name and address on the note pad. He managed to say a polite thanks and headed for the door. As he closed the door, he realized he had forgotten to leave his phone number.

When he opened the manager's door, Mr. Jenson was once again leafing carelessly through the magazine. On the corner of the desk lay a **crumpled** piece of note pad paper.

—Student

EXERCISE 1

SELF-TEST: After reading the above selection, do the following. Look at the Master Words below. Underline the words that you think you know. Circle the words that you are less sure about. Draw a square around the words you don't recognize.

MASTER WORDS

applicant	entirely	prop
crumple	maitre d'	suspicion
despair	mislead	tilt
dutiful		

Read the selection on the preceding page again, this time paying special attention to the ten Master Words. In the (a) spaces provided below, write down what you think is the meaning of the word. After you have attempted a definition for each word, look up the word in a dictionary. In the (b) spaces, copy the appropriate dictionary definition.

1. **applicant** (n.)

    a. _____

    b. ___ one who applies for or requests a job, help, etc.; a candidate ___

2. **crumple** (v.)

    a. _____

    b. ___ to crush together into folds or wrinkles; to rumple ___

3. **despair** (n.)

    a. _____

    b. ___ complete loss of hope, faith, or confidence ___

4. **dutiful** (adj.)

    a. _____

    b. ___ having a sense of duty or obligation; obedient; respectful ___

5. **entirely** (adv.)

    a. _____

    b. ___ wholly; fully; in all respects ___

6. **maitre d'** (n.)

    a. _____

    b. ___ the headwaiter in a restaurant ___

7. **mislead** (v.)

    a. _____

    b. ___ to lead into error of conduct or thought; to lead astray ___

8. **prop** (v.)

    a. _____

    b. ___ to prevent something from falling by placing something under or against it; also, to rest upon such a support ___

9. **suspicion** (n.)

    a. _____

    b. ___ the feeling that something is wrong; uneasiness; distrust ___

10. **tilt** (v.)

    a. _____

    b. ___ to cause to lean, incline, slope, or slant ___

Use the following list of synonyms and antonyms to fill in the blanks. Some words have no antonyms. In such cases, the antonym blanks have been marked with an X.

busboy	deceive	guide	lean	rebellious	support
candidate	distrust	headwaiter	obedient	smooth	tumble
completely	employer	hopelessness	partly	straighten	wrinkle
confidence	faith				

	Synonyms	**Antonyms**
1. **despair**	(hopelessness)	(faith)
2. **maitre d'**	(headwaiter)	(busboy)
3. **applicant**	(candidate)	(employer)
4. **tilt**	(lean)	(straighten)
5. **prop**	(support)	(tumble)
6. **suspicion**	(distrust)	(confidence)
7. **entirely**	(completely)	(partly)
8. **mislead**	(deceive)	(guide)
9. **dutiful**	(obedient)	(rebellious)
10. **crumple**	(wrinkle)	(smooth)

Decide whether the first pair in the items below are synonyms or antonyms. Then choose the Master Word that shows a similar relation to the word(s) preceding the blank.

1. assume	:presuppose	::slant	:	(tilt)
2. exclaim	:mumble	::flatten	:	(crumple)
3. marvel	:routine matter	::interviewer	:	(applicant)
4. expert	:untrained	::trust	:	(suspicion)
5. duplication	:reproduction	::respectful	:	(dutiful)
6. antics	:pranks	::brace	:	(prop)
7. pattern	:model	::totally	:	(entirely)
8. junction	:crossroads	::chief waiter	:	(maitre d')
9. intersect	:crisscross	::misinform	:	(mislead)
10. posse	:fugitive	::hope	:	(despair)

The Master Words in this lesson are repeated below. From the Master Words, choose the appropriate word for the blank in each of the following sentences. Write the word in the numbered space provided at the right.

applicant	despair	entirely	mislead	suspicion
crumple	dutiful	maitre d'	prop	tilt

1. Bob nervously realized that he was not the only ...?... for the job.

1. __(applicant)__

2. The couple was disappointed that the ...?... had not seated them near a window.

2. __(maitre d')__

3. After searching the closet, I finally found my favorite blouse ...?...(d, ed) on the floor.

3. __(crumple)__

4. The Leaning Tower of Pisa is famous because its poor foundation caused it to ...?... even before it was completely built.

4. __(tilt)__

5. The ...?... of the fans was obvious as their team lost its fourth game in a row.

5. __(despair)__

6. Kevin brought two books to ...?... up the movie projector so the image on the screen would be square.

6. __(prop)__

7. Advertising often ...?...(s) consumers into thinking that a particular product will solve many problems.

7. __(mislead)__

8. The ...?... dog would sit for hours on command.

8. __(dutiful)__

9. The con man first roused my ...?... by insisting that he had to have cash for his goods.

9. __(suspicion)__

10. Her arguments weren't ...?... convincing, so he asked for more proof.

10. __(entirely)__

To complete this puzzle, fill in the Master Word associated with each phrase below. Then unscramble the circled letters to form a Master Word from Lesson 7, and define it.

1. what clothes do if you sleep in them   c r u m p l e

2. you have this if you "smell a rat"   s u s p i (c) i o n

3. what some book covers do   m i s l e (a) d

4. loyal and considerate   d u (t) i f u l

5. tell this person if the service isn't good   m a (i) t r e d'

6. result of being "down in the dumps"   d e (s) p a i r

7. one hundred percent   e (n) t i r e l y

8. future employee, perhaps   a p p l i c a n t

9. to rest against   p r o p

10. how to straighten a crooked picture   t i l t

Unscrambled word: __(antics)__

Definition: __(wild or funny actions, often engaged in to get attention)__

(Note: Definition may vary.)

Read the following selection to get the general meaning. Read it a second time, paying special attention to the words in dark type. Notice how they are used in sentences. These are Master Words. These are the words you will be working with in this lesson.

From **Cool Cat**
by Frank Bonham

At nine o'clock the next morning, Buddy sat in a deck chair before his home, gazing out over treetops and flat city blocks and **tingling** with **expectation**. In the house, he could hear Rich talking to Angie, his sister. Rich had just arrived on his motor scooter. Buddy's younger brother, Ralphie, was inside somewhere playing a music box. Buddy could hear the mindless **tinkle** of it going on steadily: "Four-and-twenty blackbirds . . ."

Buddy saw everything through an **opalescent haze** of hope, dreaming of those off-center bats of Cool's uncle's . . . just a **hunch**, that if they all let their minds stretch a little, they'd find some moneymaking plan to move them.

From where he sat, he could see a sweep of **multicolored** tar-paper roofs. Farther out rose little hills that were part of the area known as Dogtown. This area reached for miles, an **irregular** pattern of poor neighborhoods—black, brown, white, Oriental, mixed. In the distance, factories belched out gray toadstools of smoke.

Very close behind Buddy's house towered a range of high, brushy hills. The Williams home was on a narrow street that snaked along a steep hillside. It was built on the high side of the street, so that the earth had had to be **excavated** to make room for the garage. The house was built above the garage and was set back from its flat roof, which was graveled and railed to serve as a front yard. Redwood furniture and plants in wooden tubs stood under the porch eaves.

When an automobile horn mooed like a cow, Buddy **lurched** from the chair and went to the railing above the street.

—Cool Cat by Frank Bonham. Copyright 1971 by Frank Bonham. E. P. Dutton and Co., Publishers.

EXERCISE 1

SELF-TEST: After reading the above selection, do the following. Look at the Master Words below. Underline the words that you think you know. Circle the words that you are less sure about. Draw a square around the words you don't recognize.

MASTER WORDS

excavate	**lurch**
expectation	**multicolored**
haze	**opalescent**
hunch	**tingle**
irregular	**tinkle**

Read the selection on the preceding page again, this time paying special attention to the ten Master Words. In the (a) spaces provided below, write down what you think is the meaning of the word. After you have attempted a definition for each word, look up the word in a dictionary. In the (b) spaces, copy the appropriate dictionary definition.

1. **excavate** (v.)

   a. _____

   b. ___ to hollow out; to dig out _____

2. **expectation** (n.)

   a. _____

   b. ___ an eager anticipation of an event _____

3. **haze** (n.)

   a. _____

   b. ___ a clouded mental state; a slight fog, mist, or smoke in the air ___

4. **hunch** (n.)

   a. _____

   b. ___ a strong feeling, often not based on facts, that something will happen ___

5. **irregular** (adj.)

   a. _____

   b. ___ not conforming to an expected pattern; lacking evenness and balance ___

6. **lurch** (v.)

   a. _____

   b. ___ to roll or sway suddenly _____

7. **multicolored** (adj.)

   a. _____

   b. ___ consisting of many colors _____

8. **opalescent** (adj.)

   a. _____

   b. ___ like a rainbow; reflecting an iridescent light ___

9. **tingle** (v.)

   a. _____

   b. ___ to feel a stinging, prickling, or thrilling sensation ___

10. **tinkle** (n.)

   a. _____

   b. ___ a short, light, ringing sound _____

Use the following list of synonyms and antonyms to fill in the blanks. Some words have no antonyms. In such cases, the antonym blanks have been marked with an X.

balanced	colorful	dig	hope	mist	sting
certainty	colorless	fill	jerk	monochrome	suspicion
clang	despair	glide	jingle	rainbow-colored	uneven
clear					

	Synonyms	**Antonyms**
1. **tingle**	(sting)	X
2. **expectation**	(hope)	(despair)
3. **tinkle**	(jingle)	(clang)
4. **opalescent**	(rainbow-colored) (colorful)	(colorless) (monochrome)
5. **haze**	(mist)	(clear)
6. **hunch**	(suspicion)	(certainty)
7. **multicolored**	(colorful) (rainbow-colored)	(monochrome) (colorless)
8. **irregular**	(uneven)	(balanced)
9. **excavate**	(dig)	(fill)
10. **lurch**	(jerk)	(glide)

Decide whether the first pair in the items below are synonyms or antonyms. Then choose the Master Word that shows a similar relation to the word(s) preceding the blank.

1. tilt	:tip	::stagger	: (lurch)
2. crumple	:straighten	::single-hued	: (multicolored)
3. applicant	:interviewee	::fog	: (haze)
4. suspicion	:certainty	::orderly	: (irregular)
5. prop	:reinforce	::eagerness	: (expectation)
6. dutiful	:disobedient	::gong	: (tinkle)
7. entirely	:fully	::guess	: (hunch)
8. despair	:trust	::bury	: (excavate)
9. maitre d'	:chief server	::shimmering	: (opalescent)
10. mislead	:fool	::prickle	: (tingle)

The Master Words in this lesson are repeated below. From the Master Words, choose the appropriate word for the blank in each of the following sentences. Write the word in the numbered space provided at the right.

| excavate | haze | irregular | multicolored | tingle |
| expectation | hunch | lurch | opalescent | tinkle |

1. While most of the flags in the world are ...?..., that island nation has a plain green banner.

1. _____(multicolored)_____

2. Clothing which is flawed in some way is often marked "...?..." and sold at a lower price.

2. _____(irregular)_____

3. The construction crew began to ...?... the area where the new shopping center was to be.

3. _____(excavate)_____

4. The train's sudden stop caused everyone to ...?... forward.

4. _____(lurch)_____

5. The children delighted in the brief ...?... splendor of the soap bubbles they were blowing.

5. _____(opalescent)_____

6. The trees and buildings looked blurred and fuzzy in the early morning ...?... .

6. _____(haze)_____

7. The ...?... of bells whenever the door opened told the shopkeeper that a customer had entered her shop.

7. _____(tinkle)_____

8. Coach Bronson had great ...?...(s) for our team; he believed we could win the conference championship.

8. _____(expectation)_____

9. Mary's cheek was numb as she left the dentist's office, but as the pain-killer wore off, her face began to ...?... .

9. _____(tingle)_____

10. Jim had (a, an) ...?... he had taken a wrong turn when the houses became fewer and fewer.

10. _____(hunch)_____

Order the words in each item from *least* to *most*. Use the abbreviations L for "least" and M for "most." Leave the line before the word of the middle degree blank. The first word provides a clue about how to arrange the words. See the example.

satisfied: _L_pleased _M_thrilled ____delighted
(*Pleased* indicates the least satisfied; *thrilled* indicates the most satisfied.)

1. clumsy: ____tumble _(M)_crash _(L)_lurch

2. colorful: ____marbled _(M)_opalescent _(L)_faded

3. odd: ____irregular _(L)_normal _(M)_weird

4. loud: ____chime _(M)_clang _(L)_tinkle

5. overcast: _(M)_pea soup ____cloudy _(L)_haze

6. sure: _(M)_certainty _(L)_hunch ____probability

7. painful: ____ache _(L)_tingle _(M)_torment

8. colorful: ____tricolored _(L)_single-hued _(M)_multicolored

9. anticipation: _(L)_mild interest _(M)_yearning ____expectation

10. digging: _(M)_excavate _(L)_scratch ____furrow

(Note: In some cases, answers may vary.)

LESSON 10

Read the following selection to get the general meaning. Read it a second time, paying special attention to the words in dark type. Notice how they are used in sentences. These are Master Words. These are the words you will be working with in this lesson.

From **Kim**
by Rudyard Kipling

He moved to the end of the **veranda** to refill the heavy, **porous** clay water-jug from the **filter**.

"Do you want drink?"

Kim nodded. Lurgan Sahib, fifteen feet off, laid one hand on the jar. Next instant, it stood at Kim's elbow, full to within half an inch of the **brim**—the white cloth only showing, by a small wrinkle, where it had slid into place.

"Wah!" said Kim in most **utter** amazement. "That is magic." Lurgan Sahib's smile showed that the **compliment** had gone home.

"Throw it back."

"It will break."

"I say, throw it back."

Kim pitched it at **random**. It fell short and crashed into fifty pieces, while the water dripped through the rough veranda boarding.

"I said it would break."

"All one. Look at it. Look at the largest piece."

That lay with a sparkle of water in its curve, as if it were a star on the floor. Kim looked intently; Lurgan Sahib laid one hand gently on the **nape** of the neck, stroked it twice or thrice, and whispered: "Look! It shall come to life again, piece by piece. First the big piece shall join itself to two others on the right and the left—on the right and the left. Look!"

To save his life, Kim could not have turned his head. The light touch held him as in a **vise**, and his blood tingled pleasantly through him. There was one large piece of the jar where there had been three, and above them the shadowy outline of the entire **vessel**. He could see the veranda through it, but it was thickening and darkening with each beat of his pulse. Yet the jar—how slowly the thoughts came!—the jar had been smashed before his eyes. Another wave of prickling fire raced down his neck, as Lurgan Sahib moved his hand.

"Look! It is coming into shape," said Lurgan Sahib.

EXERCISE 1

SELF-TEST: After reading the above selection, do the following. Look at the Master Words below. Underline the words that you think you know. Circle the words that you are less sure about. Draw a square around the words you don't recognize.

MASTER WORDS

brim	random
compliment	utter
filter	veranda
nape	vessel
porous	vise

Read the selection on the preceding page again, this time paying special attention to the ten Master Words. In the (a) spaces provided below, write down what you think is the meaning of the word. After you have attempted a definition for each word, look up the word in a dictionary. In the (b) spaces, copy the appropriate dictionary definition.

1. **brim** (n.)

   a. _____

   b. _____ the upper edge or rim of a cup, glass, etc. ____

2. **compliment** (n.)

   a. _____

   b. _____ an expression of praise or admiration _____

3. **filter** (n.)

   a. _____

   b. _____ any device used to strain solid matter from liquids ___

4. **nape** (n.)

   a. _____

   b. _____ the back of the neck _____

5. **porous** (adj.)

   a. _____

   b. _____ having holes, or pores, which allow the passage of water or air ___

6. **random** (adj.)

   a. _____

   b. _____ without definite aim or purpose; haphazard ____

7. **utter** (adj.)

   a. _____

   b. _____ complete; total; absolute _____

8. **veranda** (n.)

   a. _____

   b. _____ a porch, usually roofed and sometimes partly enclosed ___

9. **vessel** (n.)

   a. _____

   b. _____ a hollow utensil such as a cup, bowl, pitcher, vase, or bottle ___

10. **vise** (n.)

   a. _____

   b. _____ a device with two jaws which may be brought together so as to hold an object while work is being done on it ___

Use the following list of synonyms and antonyms to fill in the blanks. Some words have no antonyms. In such cases, the antonym blanks have been marked with an X.

absorbent	complete	edge	porch	sealed
aimless	container	partial	praise	strainer
bottom	criticism	planned	scruff	throat
clamp				

		Synonyms	**Antonyms**
1.	**veranda**	(porch)	X
2.	**porous**	(absorbent)	(sealed)
3.	**filter**	(strainer)	X
4.	**brim**	(edge)	(bottom)
5.	**utter**	(complete)	(partial)
6.	**compliment**	(praise)	(criticism)
7.	**random**	(aimless)	(planned)
8.	**nape**	(scruff)	(throat)
9.	**vise**	(clamp)	X
10.	**vessel**	(container)	X

Decide whether the first pair in the items below are synonyms or antonyms. Then choose the Master Word that shows a similar relation to the word(s) preceding the blank.

1. multicolored	:single-hued	::waterproof	:	(porous)
2. lurch	:totter	::jug	:	(vessel)
3. haze	:cloudlessness	::limited	:	(utter)
4. expectation	:desire	::screen	:	(filter)
5. irregular	:uniform	::base	:	(brim)
6. hunch	:gut feeling	::back of neck	:	(nape)
7. opalescent	:varicolored	::grip	:	(vise)
8. tinkle	:racket	::scheduled	:	(random)
9. excavate	:cover up	::insult	:	(compliment)
10. tingle	:quiver	::terrace	:	(veranda)

The Master Words in this lesson are repeated below. From the Master Words, choose the appropriate word for the blank in each of the following sentences. Write the word in the numbered space provided at the right.

brim	filter	porous	utter	vessel
compliment	nape	random	veranda	vise

1. On the ...?... we can enjoy the sound of locusts and the smell of roses as we talk over events of the day.

1. _____ (veranda) _____

2. The ...?... nature of sponges makes them ideal for soaking up spills.

2. _____ (porous) _____

3. An important step in purifying water is to ...?... solid particles from the liquid.

3. _____ (filter) _____

4. By coincidence I found the information I was looking for by reading (a, an) ...?... passage.

4. _____ (random) _____

5. Everyone called the scientist's theory ...?... nonsense.

5. _____ (utter) _____

6. Alberto, the old glass blower, one day showed us the secret to making his beautiful, delicate ...?...(s).

6. _____ (vessel) _____

7. Afraid that she would spill coffee from the mugs filled to the ...?..., the new waitress walked gingerly across the cafe.

7. _____ (brim) _____

8. The carpenter used (a, an) ...?... to hold the piece of wood in place.

8. _____ (vise) _____

9. Linda's wool dress collar irritated the ...?... of her neck.

9. _____ (nape) _____

10. Joan was pleased with the ...?...(s) she received on her performance in the piano recital.

10. _____ (compliment) _____

The invented words below are formed from parts of different Master Words from this lesson. Create a definition and indicate the part of speech for each word. The first one is done for you.

napevise	*(n.) in first aid, a collar used to immobilize the neck*
verandom	([n.] a haphazardly built porch)
utterporous	([adj.] allowing for maximum air or water flow)
brimpliment	([n.] praise that fully satisfies another)

Now invent your own words by combining parts of the Master Words. Create a definition for each, and indicate the word's part of speech. (You may reuse any of the word parts above in new combinations.)

1. _____   _____

2. _____   _____

(Note: Answers will vary.)

Other possibilities:

brimfilter	(n.) a woven or webbed hat that filters sunlight
compliranda	(n.) a courteous greeting exchanged from a porch
utterbrim	(v.) to fill to the very top

Read the following selection to get the general meaning. Read it a second time, paying special attention to the words in dark type. Notice how they are used in sentences. These are Master Words. These are the words you will be working with in this lesson.

From **Five Little Peppers and How They Grew** by Margaret Sidney

The good times were coming for Polly—coming pretty near, and she didn't know it! All the children were in on the secret, for, as Mrs. Pepper declared, "They'd have to know it; and if they were let into the secret they'd keep it better."

So they had **individually** and **collectively** been entrusted with the precious secret and **charged** with the extreme importance of "never letting anyone know," and they had been nearly bursting ever since with the wild desire to [share] their knowledge.

"I'm afraid I *shall* tell," said David, running to his mother at last. "Oh, mammy, I don't dare stay near Polly, I do want to tell *so bad.*"

"Oh, no, you won't, David," said his mother encouragingly, "when you know mother [doesn't] want you to; and besides, think how Polly'll look when she sees it."

"I know," cried David, in the greatest **rapture**, "I wouldn't tell for all the world! I guess she'll look nice, don't you, mother?" and he laughed in **glee** at the thought.

"Poor child! I guess she will!" and then Mrs. Pepper laughed too, till the little old kitchen rang with delight at the **accustomed** sound.

The children all had to play "clap in and clap out" in the bedroom while *it* came; and "stagecoach" too. "Anything to make a noise," Ben said. And then after they got nicely started in the game, he would be missing to help about the mysterious thing in the kitchen, which was safe since Polly couldn't see him go on account of her bandage. So she didn't suspect in the least. And although the rest were almost dying to be out in the kitchen, they **conscientiously** stuck to their bargain to keep Polly occupied. Only Joel *would* open the door and **peep** once; and then Phronsie behind him began—"Oh, I see the sto—" but David **swooped** down on her in a twinkling and **smothered** the rest by tickling her.

EXERCISE 1

SELF-TEST: After reading the above selection, do the following. Look at the Master Words below. Underline the words that you think you know. Circle the words that you are less sure about. Draw a square around the words you don't recognize.

MASTER WORDS

accustomed	individual
charge	peep
collective	rapture
conscientious	smother
glee	swoop

Read the selection on the preceding page again, this time paying special attention to the ten Master Words. In the (a) spaces provided below, write down what you think is the meaning of the word. After you have attempted a definition for each word, look up the word in a dictionary. In the (b) spaces, copy the appropriate dictionary definition.

1. **accustomed** (adj.)

   a. _____

   b. _____ customary; usual; habitual; familiar through use or repeated experience

2. **charge** (v.)

   a. _____

   b. _____ to trust with a responsibility or duty; to place a load or burden upon

3. **collective** (adj.)

   a. _____

   b. _____ having to do with a group of individuals viewed as a whole; mass; sum

4. **conscientious** (adj.)

   a. _____

   b. _____ controlled by one's conscience or one's sense of right; just; upright; careful

5. **glee** (n.)

   a. _____

   b. _____ joy; merriment; exultation; delight

6. **individual** (adj.)

   a. _____

   b. _____ involving or concerning a single person or thing; particular; separate

7. **peep** (v.)

   a. _____

   b. _____ to look at slyly or secretly, especially through a small opening

8. **rapture** (n.)

   a. _____

   b. _____ extreme joy or delight; ecstasy

9. **smother** (v.)

   a. _____

   b. _____ to hide by covering up; to suppress; to suffocate

10. **swoop** (v.)

    a. _____

    b. _____ to descend suddenly, often in an attack

Use the following list of synonyms and antonyms to fill in the blanks. Some words have no antonyms. In such cases, the antonym blanks have been marked with an X.

burden	despondence	joint	peek	separate	suppress
careful	dive	mirth	relieve	single	untypical
careless	encourage	overjoyfulness	rise	sorrow	usual
combined	gaze				

	Synonyms	**Antonyms**
1. **individual**	(separate) (single)	(joint) (combined)
2. **collective**	(combined) (joint)	(single) (separate)
3. **charge**	(burden)	(relieve)
4. **rapture**	(overjoyfulness)	(despondence) (sorrow)
5. **glee**	(mirth)	(sorrow) (despondence)
6. **accustomed**	(usual)	(untypical)
7. **conscientious**	(careful)	(careless)
8. **peep**	(peek)	(gaze)
9. **swoop**	(dive)	(rise)
10. **smother**	(suppress)	(encourage)

Decide whether the first pair in the items below are synonyms or antonyms. Then choose the Master Word that shows a similar relation to the word(s) preceding the blank.

1. porous	:watertight	::reckless	:	(conscientious)
2. vessel	:jar	::glance	:	(peep)
3. utter	:slight	::fan	:	(smother)
4. filter	:sieve	::tax	:	(charge)
5. nape	:scruff	::united	:	(collective)
6. vise	:clasp	::pounce	:	(swoop)
7. random	:orderly	::sadness	:	(glee)
8. veranda	:porch	::single	:	(individual)
9. compliment	:put-down	::unfamiliar	:	(accustomed)
10. brim	:rim	::joy	:	(rapture)

EXERCISE 5

The Master Words in this lesson are repeated below. From the Master Words, choose the appropriate word for the blank in each of the following sentences. Write the word in the numbered space provided at the right.

accustomed	collective	glee	peep	smother
charge	conscientious	individual	rapture	swoop

1. The artist realized that he should not ...?... his creative ideas, no matter how wild those ideas seemed to be.

1. _____(smother)_____

2. They tried to ...?... through the fence to watch the baseball game.

2. _____(peep)_____

3. The caretaker was ...?...(d, ed) with the duty of keeping the museum safe and clean.

3. _____(charge)_____

4. The South American condor, with a wing span of twelve feet, has been known to ...?... down upon a full-grown llama.

4. _____(swoop)_____

5. Rodney's ...?... violin practice paid off when he was selected as a member of the youth orchestra.

5. _____(conscientious)_____

6. The ...?... list of demands was compiled by both groups.

6. _____(collective)_____

7. My little brother is a mischief-maker who laughs in ...?... whenever I fall for one of his practical jokes.

7. _____(glee)_____

8. Having been born in the zoo, the young lions were not ...?... to hunting their own food.

8. _____(accustomed)_____

9. Some students participate in sports; others, in music, drama, or science clubs, depending on their ...?... interests.

9. _____(individual)_____

10. When they were reunited after thirty years, the loving sisters were in a state of ...?... .

10. _____(rapture)_____

EXERCISE 6

Write the Master Word that is associated with each word group below. Then list three things that might be associated with the review word that follows.

1. hardworking, dependable, trustworthy

_____(conscientious)_____

2. crack, spy hole, keyhole

_____(peep)_____

3. load, weigh down, saddle

_____(charge)_____

4. affection, kisses, pillow

_____(smother)_____

5. hang glider, flying squirrel, eagle

_____(swoop)_____

6. victory, party, merrymaking

_____(glee)_____

7. fingerprint, one-serving meal, solo flight

_____(individual)_____

8. family, herd, team

_____(collective)_____

9. usual comforts, status quo, habits

_____(accustomed)_____

10. bliss, ecstasy, cloud nine

_____(rapture)_____

Review word: gaze (Lesson 6)

_____(birdwatchers)_____   _____(astronomers)_____   _____(daydreamers)_____

(Note: Answers may vary.)

LESSON 12

PART I: From the list below, choose the appropriate word for each sentence that follows. Use each word only once. There will be two words left over.

affirm	compliment	hunch	intent	random
coincidence	despondent	imprudent	irregular	rely
collective	distribute	individual	oblige	

1. Sometimes students _____(distribute)_____ the tests, but only the teacher gathers them up.

2. Although the television was playing and there was much activity in the room, Margaret was _____(intent)_____ on her reading.

3. Though the mayor _____(affirm)_____(d, ed) that she would cut the city budget, she did not keep her promise.

4. Many people think stockpiling nuclear weapons is _____(imprudent)_____ and dangerous.

5. Meeting our next-door neighbors by chance a thousand miles from home was indeed (a, an) _____(coincidence)_____.

6. Accepting (a, an) _____(compliment)_____ may be hard for people who tend to make light of their own achievements.

7. The chances of changing policies are greater if we make (a, an) _____(collective)_____ protest than if we act separately.

8. When ten _____(random)_____ rolls of the dice turned up ten sixes, Chris began to suspect that something more than fate was at work.

9. The _____(irregular)_____ spread of the branches left our evergreen looking bare on one side.

10. Because the road was closed for repairs, we were _____(oblige)_____(d, ed) to take a ten-mile detour.

11. Five months after Claire left him, Stuart was still _____(despondent)_____.

12. I buy from that store because I can _____(rely)_____ on their well-made products.

PART II: Decide whether the first pair in the items below are synonyms or antonyms. Then choose a Master Word from Lessons 1-11 which shows a similar relation to the word(s) preceding the blank. Do not repeat a Master Word that appears in the first column.

1. deny	:acknowledge	::polite	:	(presumptuous)
2. filter	:blender	::occasional	:	(constant)
3. expectation	:anticipation	::cloudiness	:	(haze)
4. fidgety	:restless	::bother	:	(irritate)
5. dutiful	:respectful	::familiar	:	(accustomed)

(Note: Other answers may be possible.)

PART III: From the list below, choose the appropriate word for each sentence that follows. Use each word only once. There will be three words left over.

antiseptic	attitude	disgust	immovable	ironical
applicant	blotchy	duplication	impressive	mechanical
assume	conscientious	excavate	interfere	relish

1. I _____(assume)_____ that man lives nearby since he's always walking around the neighborhood, but I'm not sure.

2. The feeding habits of the caracara, a vulture-like bird found mostly in South America, would fill most people with _____(disgust)_____.

3. Winston was (a, an) _____(conscientious)_____ worker who reported to work on time and did his best while he was on the job.

4. After Lynn ate the strawberries, _____(blotchy)_____ red patches appeared on her skin.

5. Some household cleaners contain _____(antiseptic)_____ agents which fight germs.

6. To compliment the cook on a meal that has been burned is being _____(ironical)_____.

7. Ralph was extremely discouraged when the manager told him that he was the fortieth _____(applicant)_____ for the part-time position.

8. Though Marc declared that the health warnings about smoking didn't scare him, his _____(attitude)_____ changed when his father died of lung cancer.

9. Folding a paper on which a wet ink blot appears will result in the _____(duplication)_____ of the pattern.

10. The builders brought in bulldozers to _____(excavate)_____ the land and put in the basement of the house.

11. Jon's singing is even more _____(impressive)_____ than his piano playing.

12. People particularly seem to _____(relish)_____ ice cream on a hot summer day.

PART IV: Decide whether the first pair in the items below are synonyms or antonyms. Then choose a Master Word from Lessons 1-11 which shows a similar relation to the word(s) preceding the blank. Do not repeat a Master Word that appears in the first column.

1. obstacle	:assistance	::everyday	:	(remarkable)
2. disengage	:fasten	::carry on	:	(hesitate)
3. rapture	:elation	::butt in	:	(interfere)
4. mislead	:guide	::uninformed	:	(conscious)
5. expert	:masterful	::eagerly	:	(greedily)

(Note: Other answers may be possible.)

Read the following selection to get the general meaning. Read it a second time, paying special attention to the words in dark type. Notice how they are used in sentences. These are Master Words. These are the words you will be working with in this lesson.

From **The Land of Oz**
by L. Frank Baum

The Scarecrow, with great politeness, introduced Tip and Jack Pumpkinhead, and the **latter personage** seemed to interest the Tin Woodman greatly.

"You are not very **substantial**, I must admit," said the Emperor; "but you are certainly unusual, and therefore worthy to become a member of our **select society**."

"I thank your Majesty," said Jack, **humbly**.

"I hope you are enjoying good health?" continued the Woodman.

"At present, yes," replied the Pumpkinhead, with a sigh; "but I am in constant terror of the day when I shall spoil."

"Nonsense!" said the Emperor—but in a kindly, **sympathetic** tone. "Do not, I beg of you, **dampen** today's sun with the showers of tomorrow. For before your head has time to spoil you can have it canned, and in that way it may be **preserved indefinitely**."

EXERCISE 1

SELF-TEST: After reading the above selection, do the following. Look at the Master Words below. Underline the words that you think you know. Circle the words that you are less sure about. Draw a square around the words you don't recognize.

MASTER WORDS

dampen	preserve
humble	select
indefinite	society
latter	substantial
personage	sympathetic

Read the selection on the preceding page again, this time paying special attention to the ten Master Words. In the (a) spaces provided below, write down what you think is the meaning of the word. After you have attempted a definition for each word, look up the word in a dictionary. In the (b) spaces, copy the appropriate dictionary definition.

1. **dampen** (v.)

   a. _____

   b. ___ to depress, discourage, or deaden; also, to moisten

2. **humble** (adj.)

   a. _____

   b. ___ without pride or vanity; modest; meek; lowly

3. **indefinite** (adj.)

   a. _____

   b. ___ not clearly defined or with no set limits

4. **latter** (adj.)

   a. _____

   b. ___ being the second of two things mentioned

5. **personage** (n.)

   a. _____

   b. ___ a person, especially one who is important or noteworthy

6. **preserve** (v.)

   a. _____

   b. ___ to keep safe from injury, destruction, or decay

7. **select** (adj.)

   a. _____

   b. ___ of special value or excellence; choice

8. **society** (n.)

   a. _____

   b. ___ a group of persons linked for any reason, having common traditions and interests or ends

9. **substantial** (adj.)

   a. _____

   b. ___ having body; solid; strong; firm

10. **sympathetic** (adj.)

    a. _____

    b. ___ having feelings of compassion or understanding

Use the following list of synonyms and antonyms to fill in the blanks. Some words have no antonyms. In such cases, the antonym blanks have been marked with an X.

choice	dignitary	former	limited	save	solid
commoner	discourage	individual	organization	second	understanding
critical	encourage	inferior	proud	shy	unmeasured
destroy	flimsy				

	Synonyms	**Antonyms**
1. **latter**	(second)	(former)
2. **personage**	(dignitary)	(commoner)
3. **substantial**	(solid)	(flimsy)
4. **select**	(choice)	(inferior)
5. **society**	(organization)	(individual)
6. **humble**	(shy)	(proud)
7. **sympathetic**	(understanding)	(critical)
8. **dampen**	(discourage)	(encourage)
9. **preserve**	(save)	(destroy)
10. **indefinite**	(unmeasured)	(limited)

Decide whether the first pair in the items below are synonyms or antonyms. Then choose the Master Word that shows a similar relation to the word(s) preceding the blank.

1. conscientious	:irresponsible	::motivate	: (dampen)
2. peep	:peek	::first-rate	: (select)
3. charge	:trust	::club	: (society)
4. smother	:stir up	::ruin	: (preserve)
5. glee	:gloom	::previous	: (latter)
6. collective	:joint	::strong	: (substantial)
7. swoop	:descend	::celebrity	: (personage)
8. accustomed	:new	::boastful	: (humble)
9. individual	:group	::uncaring	: (sympathetic)
10. rapture	:delight	::limitless	: (indefinite)

The Master Words in this lesson are repeated below. From the Master Words, choose the appropriate word for the blank in each of the following sentences. Write the word in the numbered space provided at the right.

| dampen | indefinite | personage | select | substantial |
| humble | latter | preserve | society | sympathetic |

1. President Lincoln was determined to ...?... the Union.

1. ___(preserve)___

2. Toby's opponent had nearly pinned him, but that did not ...?... his hopes of winning the wrestling match.

2. ___(dampen)___

3. None of the prisoners knew when they would be released because they all had been given ...?... sentences.

3. ___(indefinite)___

4. ...?...(s) from around the world came to the funeral to mourn the President's death.

4. ___(Personage)___

5. Only ...?... students were accepted as members of the Honor Society.

5. ___(select)___

6. Although the police believed Jenkins was the thief, they could find no ...?... evidence to support their suspicion.

6. ___(substantial)___

7. The Chamber of Commerce is (a, an) ...?... of businesspeople who work in the collective interest of the community.

7. ___(society)___

8. I enjoy baseball and football, but I prefer the ...?... because I once was a halfback.

8. ___(latter)___

9. Brian was extremely ...?... as he accepted the medal of heroism, saying that anyone else would have acted as he had.

9. ___(humble)___

10. A good friend knows when to give advice and when to just lend (a, an) ...?... ear.

10. ___(sympathetic)___

Fill in the chart below with the Master Word that fits each set of clues. Part of speech refers to the word's usage in the lesson. Use a dictionary when necessary.

Number of Syllables	Part of Speech	Other Clues	Master Word
3	noun	a VIP is also this	1. ___(personage)___
4	adjective	*apathetic* is its opposite	2. ___(sympathetic)___
4	adjective	the number of stars in the sky is this	3. ___(indefinite)___
2	adjective	the chosen few	4. ___(select)___
4	noun	a loner does not care for this	5. ___(society)___
2	verb	to make a pickle, you have to do this	6. ___(preserve)___
2	verb	"lay a wet blanket on"	7. ___(dampen)___
2	adjective	*arrogant* is its opposite	8. ___(humble)___
2	adjective	last-mentioned	9. ___(latter)___
3	adjective	no small thing	10. ___(substantial)___

Read the following selection to get the general meaning. Read it a second time, paying special attention to the words in dark type. Notice how they are used in sentences. These are Master Words. These are the words you will be working with in this lesson.

From **Around the World in Eighty Days**
by Jules Verne

As for Passepartout, he was a true Parisian of Paris. Since he had **abandoned** his own country for England, taking service as a **valet**, he had in vain searched for a master after his own heart. Passepartout was by no means one of these **pert dunces depicted** by Moliere, with a bold gaze and a nose held high in the air; he was an honest fellow, with a pleasant face, lips a **trifle protruding**, soft-mannered and **serviceable**, with a good round head, such as one likes to see on the shoulders of a friend. His eyes were blue, his complexion **rubicund**, his figure almost **portly** and well built, his body muscular, and his physical powers fully developed by the exercises of his younger days. His brown hair was somewhat tumbled; for while the ancient sculptors are said to have known eighteen methods of arranging Minerva's tresses, Passepartout was familiar with but one of dressing his own: three strokes of a large-tooth comb completed his [grooming].

EXERCISE 1

SELF-TEST: After reading the above selection, do the following. Look at the Master Words below. Underline the words that you think you know. Circle the words that you are less sure about. Draw a square around the words you don't recognize.

MASTER WORDS

abandon	**protrude**
depict	**rubicund**
dunce	**serviceable**
pert	**trifle**
portly	**valet**

Read the selection on the preceding page again, this time paying special attention to the ten Master Words. In the (a) spaces provided below, write down what you think is the meaning of the word. After you have attempted a definition for each word, look up the word in a dictionary. In the (b) spaces, copy the appropriate dictionary definition.

1. **abandon** (v.)

   a. _____

   b. ___ to leave, especially completely and forever; to forsake ___

2. **depict** (v.)

   a. _____

   b. ___ to give a picture of, often by use of words; to portray; to describe ___

3. **dunce** (n.)

   a. _____

   b. ___ a dull-witted or stupid person ___

4. **pert** (adj.)

   a. _____

   b. ___ bold; forward; lively; sassy ___

5. **portly** (adj.)

   a. _____

   b. ___ large in body; stout ___

6. **protrude** (v.)

   a. _____

   b. ___ to stick out; to project ___

7. **rubicund** (adj.)

   a. _____

   b. ___ reddish or ruddy in complexion ___

8. **serviceable** (adj.)

   a. _____

   b. ___ fit for performing a duty; useful ___

9. **trifle** (n.)

   a. _____

   b. ___ a little bit; a matter of small importance or value ___

10. **valet** (n.)

    a. _____

    b. ___ a servant or attendant who takes care of the clothing and grooming of an employer or customers ___

Use the following list of synonyms and antonyms to fill in the blanks. Some words have no antonyms. In such cases, the antonym blanks have been marked with an X.

bit	genius	pale	reddish	servant	timid
describe	master	project	remain	slim	useful
desert	misrepresent	recede	sassy	stout	useless
fool	much				

	Synonyms	**Antonyms**
1. **abandon**	(desert)	(remain)
2. **valet**	(servant)	(master)
3. **pert**	(sassy)	(timid)
4. **dunce**	(fool)	(genius)
5. **depict**	(describe)	(misrepresent)
6. **trifle**	(bit)	(much)
7. **protrude**	(project)	(recede)
8. **serviceable**	(useful)	(useless)
9. **rubicund**	(reddish)	(pale)
10. **portly**	(stout)	(slim)

Decide whether the first pair in the items below are synonyms or antonyms. Then choose the Master Word that shows a similar relation to the word(s) preceding the blank.

1. dampen	:hearten	::plenty	: (trifle)
2. select	:chosen	::handy	: (serviceable)
3. society	:community	::leave	: (abandon)
4. substantial	:sturdy	::picture	: (depict)
5. personage	:public figure	::rude	: (pert)
6. preserve	:protect	::simpleton	: (dunce)
7. latter	:first	::dent	: (protrude)
8. humble	:conceited	::thin	: (portly)
9. sympathetic	:unfeeling	::employer	: (valet)
10. indefinite	:unclear	::rosy	: (rubicund)

The Master Words in this lesson are repeated below. From the Master Words, choose the appropriate word for the blank in each of the following sentences. Write the word in the numbered space provided at the right.

| abandon | dunce | portly | rubicund | trifle |
| depict | pert | protrude | serviceable | valet |

1. Outdoor life gave many of the pioneers (a, an) ...?... complexion.

1. _(rubicund)_____

2. Polly was pleased to learn that the tiny glass animals she had admired cost only (a, an) ...?... .

2. _(trifle)_____

3. The ...?... man waddled toward the chocolate bar.

3. _(portly)_____

4. Mark Twain vividly ...?...(d, ed) boyhood life along the Mississippi River in many of his stories and books.

4. _(depict)_____

5. When Elaine spilled sauce on her jacket, she gave it to the hotel ...?... to clean.

5. _(valet)_____

6. In a compound fracture, a broken bone may ...?... through the skin.

6. _(protrude)_____

7. Everyone believed that Jack was able to do good work; no one could understand why he pretended to be a ...?... .

7. _(dunce)_____

8. The ...?... child did not hesitate to tell the hostess that the meat was tough and the vegetables too salty.

8. _(pert)_____

9. The old sea captain refused to ...?... his ship, even when it was obvious that the vessel was sinking.

9. _(abandon)_____

10. My ...?... car may not be sporty, but it always starts in the winter.

10. _(serviceable)_____

To complete the word spiral, choose the Master Word associated with each phrase below. Start with 1 and fill in each answer clockwise. Be careful! Each new word may overlap the previous word by one or more letters.

1. personal attendant

2. just a smidgen

3. after jogging, your face may look like this

4. a slow-witted person might be called this

5. leave behind for good

6. smart-alecky

7. radios and blow-dryers are this

8. noses and ski jumps do this

9. paint a picture or describe

10. a hefty person is this

1. V	A	L	E	2. T	R	I	F
O	N	6. P	E	R	T	7. S	L
D	T	R	U	9. D	E	E	E
N	O	T	L	Y	P	R	3. R
A	R	R			I	V	U
B	8. P	O	10. P	T	C	I	B
5. A	E	L	B	A	E	C	I
E	C	N	U	4. D	N	U	C

Read the following selection to get the general meaning. Read it a second time, paying special attention to the words in dark type. Notice how they are used in sentences. These are Master Words. These are the words you will be working with in this lesson.

Adapted from **Black Beauty**
by Anna Sewell

I went on the stand at eight in the morning, and had done a good share of work, when we had to take a fare to the railway. A long train was just expected in, so my driver pulled up at the back of some of the outside cabs to take the chance of a return fare. It was a very heavy train, and as all the cabs were soon **engaged** ours was called for. There was a party of four; a noisy, **blustery** man with a lady, a little boy and a young girl, and a great deal of luggage. The lady and the boy got into the cab, and while the man ordered about the luggage the young girl came and looked at me.

"Papa," she said, "I am sure this poor horse cannot take us and all our luggage so far, he is so very weak and worn out. Do look at him."

"Oh! he's all right, miss," said my driver, "he's strong enough."

"Papa, papa, do take a second cab," said the young girl in a **beseeching** tone. "I am sure we are wrong, I am sure it is very cruel."

"Nonsense, Grace, get in at once, and don't make all this fuss."

My gentle friend had to obey, and box after box was dragged up and **lodged** on the top of the cab or settled by the side of the driver. At last all was ready, and with his usual jerk at the rein and **slash** of the whip he drove out of the station.

The load was very heavy and I had had neither food nor rest since morning; but I did my best, as I always had done, in spite of cruelty and **injustice**.

I got along fairly till we came to Ludgate Hill, but there the heavy load and my own **exhaustion** were too much. I was struggling to keep on, **goaded** by constant **chucks** of the rein and use of the whip, when in a single moment—I cannot tell how—my feet slipped from under me, and I fell heavily to the ground on my side; the suddenness and the force with which I fell seemed to beat all the breath out of my body. I thought I heard that sweet, **pitiful** voice saying, "Oh! that poor horse! It is all our fault."

EXERCISE 1

SELF-TEST: After reading the above selection, do the following. Look at the Master Words below. Underline the words that you think you know. Circle the words that you are less sure about. Draw a square around the words you don't recognize.

MASTER WORDS

beseech	**goad**
blustery	**injustice**
chuck	**lodge**
engaged	**pitiful**
exhaustion	**slash**

Read the selection on the preceding page again, this time paying special attention to the ten Master Words. In the (a) spaces provided below, write down what you think is the meaning of the word. After you have attempted a definition for each word, look up the word in a dictionary. In the (b) spaces, copy the appropriate dictionary definition.

1. **beseech** (v.)

   a. _____

   b. _____ to beg, implore, appeal, or plead _____

2. **blustery** (adj.)

   a. _____

   b. _____ roaring, violent, as a strong wind or an angry person, often making empty threats; boisterous

3. **chuck** (n.)

   a. _____

   b. _____ a light tap or pat, especially under the chin

4. **engaged** (adj.)

   a. _____

   b. _____ busy; occupied; involved _____

5. **exhaustion** (n.)

   a. _____

   b. _____ extreme weakness, fatigue, or weariness

6. **goad** (v.)

   a. _____

   b. _____ to spur on or urge on; to stimulate

7. **injustice** (n.)

   a. _____

   b. _____ unjust or unfair treatment or deed; wrong

8. **lodge** (v.)

   a. _____

   b. _____ to place firmly in a particular position; to embed

9. **pitiful** (adj.)

   a. _____

   b. _____ deserving of compassion, sympathy, or pity

10. **slash** (n.)

   a. _____

   b. _____ a sweeping, cutting motion

Use the following list of synonyms and antonyms to fill in the blanks. Some words have no antonyms. In such cases, the antonym blanks have been marked with an X.

available	enviable	pathetic	quiet	right	tap
cut	grant	pep	remove	spur	unfairness
embed	occupied	plead	restrain	stormy	weariness

	Synonyms	**Antonyms**
1. **engaged**	(occupied)	(available)
2. **blustery**	(stormy)	(quiet)
3. **beseech**	(plead)	(grant)
4. **lodge**	(embed)	(remove)
5. **slash**	(cut)	X
6. **injustice**	(unfairness)	(right)
7. **exhaustion**	(weariness)	(pep)
8. **goad**	(spur)	(restrain)
9. **chuck**	(tap)	X
10. **pitiful**	(pathetic)	(enviable)

Decide whether the first pair in the items below are synonyms or antonyms. Then choose the Master Word that shows a similar relation to the word(s) preceding the blank.

1. trifle	:sizable	::give	: (beseech)
2. serviceable	:helpful	::pat	: (chuck)
3. dunce	:scholar	::energy	: (exhaustion)
4. abandon	:depart	::place	: (lodge)
5. protrude	:indent	::calm	: (blustery)
6. depict	:represent	::wrong	: (injustice)
7. pert	:outspoken	::stroke	: (slash)
8. portly	:slender	::free	: (engaged)
9. valet	:attendant	::heartbreaking	: (pitiful)
10. rubicund	:reddish	::urge	: (goad)

The Master Words in this lesson are repeated below. From the Master Words, choose the appropriate word for the blank in each of the following sentences. Write the word in the numbered space provided at the right.

beseech	chuck	exhaustion	injustice	pitiful
blustery	engaged	goad	lodge	slash

1. Some people believe that a great ...?... was done to the American Indians and that the government should right the old wrongs.

1. _____ (injustice)

2. Fred was ...?...(d, ed) into taking the dare against his better judgment.

2. _____ (goad)

3. Most young animals enjoy a playful ...?... under the chin.

3. _____ (chuck)

4. After searching all over the yard for the lost Frisbee, we finally found it ...?...(d, ed) in the apple tree.

4. _____ (lodge)

5. Mark was accustomed to running a mile every day, but after the five-mile race, he was overcome with ...?... .

5. _____ (exhaustion)

6. The prisoner wept and ...?...(d, ed) the queen to believe his story, but she refused to hear his plea.

6. _____ (beseech)

7. Mr. Kramer is (a, an) ...?... man who often scolds his class in a loud voice but rarely carries out his threats.

7. _____ (blustery)

8. We couldn't meet in the library because it was already ...?... .

8. _____ (engaged)

9. The ...?... face of the lost dog touched Mother's heart, and she gave him a few scraps of meat.

9. _____ (pitiful)

10. Daniel Boone ...?...(d, ed) a trail through the unexplored wilderness of Kentucky.

10. _____ (slash)

The invented words below are formed from parts of different Master Words from this lesson. Create a definition and indicate the part of speech for each word. The first one is done for you.

engagoad _(v.) to push someone to become more involved_

goadchuck ([n.] a light pat under the chin intended to provoke another)

blusterseech ([v.] to beg violently or angrily)

slashaustion ([n.] fatigue brought on by use of a machete)

Now invent your own words by combining parts of the Master Words. Create a definition for each, and indicate the word's part of speech. (You may reuse any of the word parts above in new combinations.)

1. _____ _____

2. _____ _____

(Note: Answers will vary.)

Other possibilities:

goadseech   (v.) to beg or plead persuasively
pitiseech   (v.) to beg in a heartbreaking manner
slashlodge   (v.) to embed a blade (as of a knife or machete) into something

LESSON 16

Read the following selection to get the general meaning. Read it a second time, paying special attention to the words in dark type. Notice how they are used in sentences. These are Master Words. These are the words you will be working with in this lesson.

From **The Log of a Cowboy**
by Andy Adams

We held the wagon and saddle horses in the rear, and when we were half a mile away from the trail **ford**, cut off about two hundred head of the leaders and started for the crossing, leaving only the horse **wrangler** and one man with the herd. On reaching the river we gave them an extra push, and the cattle **plunged** into the muddy water. Before the cattle had advanced fifty feet, **instinct** warned them of the **treacherous** footing, and the leaders tried to turn back; but by that time we had the entire bunch in the water and were urging them forward. They had halted but a moment and begun **milling**, when several heavy steers sank; then we gave way and allowed the rest to come back. We did not realize fully the treachery of this river until we saw that twenty cattle were caught in the **merciless** grasp of the quicksand. They sank slowly to the level of their bodies, which gave sufficient **resistance** to support their weight, but they were hopelessly **bogged**. We allowed the free cattle to return to the herd, and immediately turned our attention to those that were bogged, some of whom were nearly **submerged** by water.

EXERCISE 1

SELF-TEST: After reading the above selection, do the following. Look at the Master Words below. Underline the words that you think you know. Circle the words that you are less sure about. Draw a square around the words you don't recognize.

MASTER WORDS

bogged	**plunge**
ford	**resistance**
instinct	**submerge**
merciless	**treacherous**
mill	**wrangler**

Read the selection on the preceding page again, this time paying special attention to the ten Master Words. In the (a) spaces provided below, write down what you think is the meaning of the word. After you have attempted a definition for each word, look up the word in a dictionary. In the (b) spaces, copy the appropriate dictionary definition.

1. **bogged** (v.)

   a. _____

   b. _____ to be sunk, as in wet, spongy ground _____

2. **ford** (n.)

   a. _____

   b. _____ a place where a body of water may be crossed by wading _____

3. **instinct** (n.)

   a. _____

   b. _____ a natural impulse, especially in animals, which leads them to act without conscious thought; unlearned behavior _____

4. **merciless** (adj.)

   a. _____

   b. _____ lacking compassion or forgiveness; cruel; harsh _____

5. **mill** (v.)

   a. _____

   b. _____ to move around in a confused or disorderly way _____

6. **plunge** (v.)

   a. _____

   b. _____ to dive or thrust forcibly or suddenly, especially into a liquid _____

7. **resistance** (n.)

   a. _____

   b. _____ a force which opposes or slows down a body or another force _____

8. **submerge** (v.)

   a. _____

   b. _____ to cover, as by water _____

9. **treacherous** (adj.)

   a. _____

   b. _____ not dependable; not to be trusted; deceptive; unreliable _____

10. **wrangler** (n.)

   a. _____

   b. _____ one who herds cows or horses _____

EXERCISE 3

Use the following list of synonyms and antonyms to fill in the blanks. Some words have no antonyms. In such cases, the antonym blanks have been marked with an X.

churn	cruel	dunk	kind	released	swamped
cowboy	dependable	emerge	learning	rise	unreliable
crossing	dive	impulse	opposition	submission	

	Synonyms	**Antonyms**
1. **ford**	(crossing)	X
2. **wrangler**	(cowboy)	X
3. **plunge**	(dive)	(rise)
4. **instinct**	(impulse)	(learning)
5. **treacherous**	(unreliable)	(dependable)
6. **mill**	(churn)	X
7. **merciless**	(cruel)	(kind)
8. **resistance**	(opposition)	(submission)
9. **bogged**	(swamped)	(released)
10. **submerge**	(dunk)	(emerge)

EXERCISE 4

Decide whether the first pair in the items below are synonyms or antonyms. Then choose the Master Word that shows a similar relation to the word(s) preceding the blank.

1. beseech	:command	::forgiving	: (merciless)
2. exhaustion	:liveliness	::loosed	: (bogged)
3. chuck	:poke	::sink	: (submerge)
4. blustery	:cool-headed	::training	: (instinct)
5. lodge	:plant	::circle	: (mill)
6. engaged	:unattached	::surface	: (plunge)
7. injustice	:mistreatment	::ranch hand	: (wrangler)
8. slash	:slice	::obstacle	: (resistance)
9. pitiful	:desirable	::safe	: (treacherous)
10. goad	:prod	::water passage	: (ford)

The Master Words in this lesson are repeated below. From the Master Words, choose the appropriate word for the blank in each of the following sentences. Write the word in the numbered space provided at the right.

bogged	instinct	mill	resistance	treacherous
ford	merciless	plunge	submerge	wrangler

1. We found a shallow place in the river that would serve as (a, an) ...?... where we could cross.

1. _____(ford)_____

2. Hans feared he would become stuck in the swamp because the ground offered no ...?... .

2. _____(resistance)_____

3. Although the walrus is not a fish but a mammal, it is able to remain ...?...(d, ed) for about twenty minutes.

3. _____(submerge)_____

4. For about an hour the young people declined to dance and just ...?...(d, ed) around the dance floor.

4. _____(mill)_____

5. The ...?... ruler put even innocent babies to death.

5. _____(merciless)_____

6. It is (a, an) ...?... of spiders to build webs.

6. _____(instinct)_____

7. When we pulled to the side of the road during the flash flood, our tires became ...?... in the soft shoulder.

7. _____(bogged)_____

8. One of the most exciting events in the life of a Texas ...?... was the long drive north on the Chisholm Trail.

8. _____(wrangler)_____

9. Suddenly the ...?... ice gave way, plunging us waist-deep into the water.

9. _____(treacherous)_____

10. The penguin waddled to the water's edge, then ...?...(d, ed) head-first to the bottom of the tank.

10. _____(plunge)_____

Order the words in each item from *least* to *most*. Use the abbreviations *L* for "least" and *M* for "most." Leave the line before the word of the middle degree blank. The first word provides a clue about how to arrange the words. See the example.

uncomfortable: ____pained __M__miserable __L__uneasy

(*Uneasy* indicates the least uncomfortable; *miserable* indicates the most uncomfortable.)

1. cruel:	____mean	__(L)__pert	__(M)__merciless
2. changeable:	____stability	__(M)__flexibility	__(L)__resistance
3. blocked:	__(M)__bogged	__(L)__slowed	____hindered
4. tightly packed:	__(M)__crush	____crowd	__(L)__mill
5. training:	__(M)__drilling	__(L)__instinct	____guidance
6. wet:	____dip	__(L)__sprinkle	__(M)__submerge
7. immersed:	__(M)__plunge	____dip	__(L)__float
8. elevated:	____low-water bridge	__(L)__ford	__(M)__overpass
9. authority:	____wrangler	__(L)__groom	__(M)__ranch owner
10. dangerous:	__(M)__treacherous	__(L)__questionable	____tricky

(Note: In some cases, answers may vary.)

Read the following selection to get the general meaning. Read it a second time, paying special attention to the words in dark type. Notice how they are used in sentences. These are Master Words. These are the words you will be working with in this lesson.

Adapted from **"The Happy Prince"**
by Oscar Wilde

High above the city, on a tall **pedestal**, stood the statue of the Happy Prince. He was **gilded** all over with thin leaves of fine gold; for eyes he had two bright **sapphires**, and a large red ruby glowed on his sword-hilt.

He was very much admired indeed. "He is as beautiful as a [weathervane]," remarked one of the Town **Councilors** who wished to gain a **reputation** for having artistic tastes; "only not quite so useful," he added, fearing that people should think him **impractical**, which he really was not.

"Why can't you be like the Happy Prince?" asked a **sensible** mother of her little boy who was crying for the Moon. "The Happy Prince never dreams of crying for anything."

"I am glad there is someone in the world who is quite happy," **muttered** a disappointed man as he gazed at the wonderful statue.

"He looks just like an angel," said the Charity Children as they came out of the cathedral in their bright scarlet **cloaks** and their clean white pinafores.

"How do you know?" said the Mathematical Master. "You have never seen one."

"Ah! but we have, in our dreams," answered the children; and the Mathematical Master frowned and looked very **severe**, for he did not approve of children dreaming.

EXERCISE 1

SELF-TEST: After reading the above selection, do the following. Look at the Master Words below. Underline the words that you think you know. Circle the words that you are less sure about. Draw a square around the words you don't recognize.

MASTER WORDS

cloak	pedestal
councilor	reputation
gilded	sapphire
impractical	sensible
mutter	severe

Read the selection on the preceding page again, this time paying special attention to the ten Master Words. In the (a) spaces provided below, write down what you think is the meaning of the word. After you have attempted a definition for each word, look up the word in a dictionary. In the (b) spaces, copy the appropriate dictionary definition.

1. **cloak** (n.)

   a. _____

   b. ___ a loose outer garment, usually without sleeves; cape

2. **councilor** (n.)

   a. _____

   b. ___ a member of a group that makes laws, gives advice, or manages government

3. **gilded** (adj.)

   a. _____

   b. ___ coated with a thin layer of gold

4. **impractical** (adj.)

   a. _____

   b. ___ unrealistic or idealistic

5. **mutter** (v.)

   a. _____

   b. ___ to speak unclearly or in a low tone, often complaining

6. **pedestal** (n.)

   a. _____

   b. ___ a base or support, especially of a statue or pillar

7. **reputation** (n.)

   a. _____

   b. ___ the opinion held of a person by others, sometimes different from the person's real character

8. **sapphire** (n.)

   a. _____

   b. ___ a precious gem deep blue in color

9. **sensible** (adj.)

   a. _____

   b. ___ having common sense or good judgment; intelligent; reasonable

10. **severe** (adj.)

   a. _____

   b. ___ strict; stern; harsh

Use the following list of synonyms and antonyms to fill in the blanks. Some words have no antonyms. In such cases, the antonym blanks have been marked with an X.

anonymity	cape	gentle	official	top
base	fame	gold-coated	reasonable	unrealistic
blue gem	foolish	grumble	stern	wise

	Synonyms	**Antonyms**
1. **pedestal**	(base)	(top)
2. **gilded**	(gold-coated)	X
3. **sapphire**	(blue gem)	X
4. **councilor**	(official)	X
5. **reputation**	(fame)	(anonymity)
6. **impractical**	(unrealistic) (foolish)	(reasonable) (wise)
7. **sensible**	(wise) (reasonable)	(foolish) (unrealistic)
8. **mutter**	(grumble)	X
9. **cloak**	(cape)	X
10. **severe**	(stern)	(gentle)

Decide whether the first pair in the items below are synonyms or antonyms. Then choose the Master Word that shows a similar relation to the word(s) preceding the blank.

1. merciless	:understanding	::head	: (pedestal)
2. submerge	:immerse	::robe	: (cloak)
3. mill	:wander	::murmur	: (mutter)
4. wrangler	:herder	::blue gem	: (sapphire)
5. bogged	:freed	::down-to-earth	: (impractical)
6. resistance	:barrier	::gold-plated	: (gilded)
7. instinct	:instruction	::kind	: (severe)
8. ford	:pass	::name	: (reputation)
9. plunge	:float	::unwise	: (sensible)
10. treacherous	:deceptive	::representative	: (councilor)

The Master Words in this lesson are repeated below. From the Master Words, choose the appropriate word for the blank in each of the following sentences. Write the word in the numbered space provided at the right.

cloak	gilded	mutter	reputation	sensible
councilor	impractical	pedestal	sapphire	severe

1. The light weight of the statue clued Marissa that it was not solid gold, just ...?... .

1. _____ (gilded) _____

2. Some colleges have a fine ...?... that they have not lived up to for many years.

2. _____ (reputation) _____

3. The class had many ideas for money-making projects, but unfortunately they were all ...?... .

3. _____ (impractical) _____

4. In most Hollywood versions of *Dracula,* the count wears a cape or (a, an) ...?... .

4. _____ (cloak) _____

5. Michigan winters, with their snow, ice, and bitter cold, are very ...?... .

5. _____ (severe) _____

6. Many of the town ...?...(s) believed the community's sewer system needed repairs.

6. _____ (councilor) _____

7. The statue of General Grant on horseback was mounted on a six-foot ...?... .

7. _____ (pedestal) _____

8. When wished a merry Christmas, Ebenezer Scrooge was known to ...?..., "Bah! Humbug!"

8. _____ (mutter) _____

9. The setting of the ring included a deep-blue ...?... .

9. _____ (sapphire) _____

10. Benjamin Franklin's *Poor Richard's Almanac* offers some ...?..., practical guidelines for living.

10. _____ (sensible) _____

Use at least five Master Words from this lesson to write a scene about one of the following topics. Or create a topic of your own. Write your choice on the blank. Circle the Master Words as you use them.

Possible Topics: Mishap at the Museum, Field Trip Mix-up

_____

_____

_____

_____

_____

_____

_____

(Note: Answers will vary.)

Read the following selection to get the general meaning. Read it a second time, paying special attention to the words in dark type. Notice how they are used in sentences. These are Master Words. These are the words you will be working with in this lesson.

From **"First Jump"**
by Henry Gregor Felsen

Ab got up. The plane was almost empty now. Only those who hadn't dared make the jump were still on board. Ab walked back and stood by the open hatch. He nodded mechanically as he heard the last instructions.

"Jump."

Ab took a deep breath. He wanted to step back, to run back to his seat. Far below him the world was turning slowly. It was so far away— so very far. He **clenched** his fists and dove out head first.

He was dropping. The wind rushed by, tearing at his nostrils. He tried to breathe, but couldn't. He was turning over and over. Above him he caught a brief **glimpse** of the transport, circling lazily around. Then he turned to see the ground rushing up at him.

He would have **yowled** in terror if he had had any breath to yowl with. He was dropping— dropping—

He remembered he had forgotten to count as he fell. What matter. Grasping **desperately**, he fought to find his ripcord. His fingernails tore against the flying suit as he clawed for it. Then his fingers closed around the metal ring and he pulled with all his strength.

It wasn't going to open! He was still falling, twisting, turning, **hurtling** toward the earth.

He **scrambled** madly to find the ripcord for his **reserve** pack. He couldn't find it. His twisting body was dropping so fast it almost whistled as it fell. He **flailed** around in despair as he prepared to smash into the ground.

Suddenly he was snapped upright. He looked up. The **chute** was spread wide, cutting his rate of **descent**. He was swinging and falling slowly.

Ab almost cried with relief. He pulled at his lines to drift toward the field. He was calm now, and enjoyed the feeling of dropping slowly. His heart was getting back to normal.

It took him a long time to get down, and finally he hit the smooth ground of the field, rolling over as he was pulled on by his chute. Ab scrambled to his feet and pulled the lines of his chute to spill the wind out of it. Then he gathered up the folds in his arms and walked toward the hangar.

They came out to meet him with a small truck. The driver laughed. "O.K., kid, you're down now."

"Huh?"

"You can let go that ripcord ring," the driver laughed. "You won't need a chute to get off the truck."

—"First Jump" by Henry Gregor Felsen. Reprinted from Boy's World , David C. Cook Publishing Co., Elgin, Ill.

EXERCISE 1

SELF-TEST: After reading the above selection, do the following. Look at the Master Words below. Underline the words that you think you know. Circle the words that you are less sure about. Draw a square around the words you don't recognize.

MASTER WORDS

chute	descent	flail	hurtle	scramble
clench	desperate	glimpse	reserve	yowl

Read the selection on the preceding page again, this time paying special attention to the ten Master Words. In the (a) spaces provided below, write down what you think is the meaning of the word. After you have attempted a definition for each word, look up the word in a dictionary. In the (b) spaces, copy the appropriate dictionary definition.

1. **chute** (n.)

   a. _____

   b. ___ an umbrella-shaped device used to slow free fall from an airplane or to slow speeding vehicles (informal for ''parachute'') ___

2. **clench** (v.)

   a. _____

   b. ___ to close tightly; also, to grasp firmly ___

3. **descent** (n.)

   a. _____

   b. ___ downward motion ___

4. **desperate** (adj.)

   a. _____

   b. ___ driven to or produced by hopelessness; reckless, rash, or frantic because of despair ___

5. **flail** (v.)

   a. _____

   b. ___ to throw one's arms or legs about wildly ___

6. **glimpse** (n.)

   a. _____

   b. ___ a hurried view ___

7. **hurtle** (v.)

   a. _____

   b. ___ to move with great speed ___

8. **reserve** (adj.)

   a. _____

   b. ___ extra, as something kept back or saved ___

9. **scramble** (v.)

   a. _____

   b. ___ to hurriedly and often clumsily struggle to get something ___

10. **yowl** (v.)

   a. _____

   b. ___ to give a long, loud, mournful cry ___

Use the following list of synonyms and antonyms to fill in the blanks. Some words have no antonyms. In such cases, the antonym blanks have been marked with an X.

clutch	dawdle	fling	howl	rise	spent
confident	extra	frantic	parachute	rush	stare
creep	fall	glance	release	scurry	whisper

	Synonyms	**Antonyms**
1. **clench**	(clutch)	(release)
2. **glimpse**	(glance)	(stare)
3. **yowl**	(howl)	(whisper)
4. **desperate**	(frantic)	(confident)
5. **hurtle**	(rush) (scurry)	(creep) (dawdle)
6. **scramble**	(scurry) (rush)	(dawdle) (creep)
7. **reserve**	(extra)	(spent)
8. **flail**	(fling)	X
9. **chute**	(parachute)	X
10. **descent**	(fall)	(rise)

Decide whether the first pair in the items below are synonyms or antonyms. Then choose the Master Word that shows a similar relation to the word(s) preceding the blank.

1. pedestal	:crown	::loosen	: (clench)
2. cloak	:coat	::parachute	: (chute)
3. impractical	:efficient	::gaze	: (glimpse)
4. severe	:tender	::climb	: (descent)
5. mutter	:mumble	::hurry	: (scramble)
6. sapphire	:blue gemstone	::bellow	: (yowl)
7. gilded	:gold-covered	::tumble	: (flail) (hurtle)
8. sensible	:romantic	::calm	: (desperate)
9. reputation	:importance	::spare	: (reserve)
10. councilor	:board member	::tumble	: (hurtle) (flail)

The Master Words in this lesson are repeated below. From the Master Words, choose the appropriate word for the blank in each of the following sentences. Write the word in the numbered space provided at the right.

| chute | descent | flail | hurtle | scramble |
| clench | desperate | glimpse | reserve | yowl |

1. The ...?... man threw all his money on the table to make one last, wild bet.

1. _____(desperate)_____

2. Even if we do drink this entire carton of milk, we have a ...?... carton in the cooler.

2. _____(reserve)_____

3. She caught a ...?... of the thief but couldn't describe him.

3. _____(glimpse)_____

4. After the quarterback fumbled, players from both teams ...?...(d, ed) to recover the loose football.

4. _____(scramble)_____

5. ...?...(s) were used to drop food and medical supplies from planes to the victims of the hurricane.

5. _____(chute)_____

6. Don's form was so good as he made his ...?... from the diving board that the judges awarded him the full ten points.

6. _____(descent)_____

7. The distant ...?... of a coyote broke the silence of the frosty, moonlit night.

7. _____(yowl)_____

8. The toddler ...?...(d, ed) the rattle tightly in his fist and shook it.

8. _____(clench)_____

9. The clown walking the tightrope ...?...(d, ed) her arms wildly and pretended to lose her balance.

9. _____(flail)_____

10. Outdistancing the other racers by 200 yards, the driver of the Porsche ...?...(d, ed) toward the finish line.

10. _____(hurtle)_____

Write the Master Word that is associated with each word group below. Then list three things that might be associated with the review word that follows.

1. starving people, last resort, emergency — _____(desperate)_____

2. space capsule, aerial acrobat, paratrooper — _____(chute)_____

3. off-balance, flapping, drowning — _____(flail)_____

4. nest egg, extra keys, spare tire — _____(reserve)_____

5. javelin, meteor, shooting star — _____(hurtle)_____

6. alarm clock, race, fire drill — _____(scramble)_____

7. plane landing, waterfall, sky diver — _____(descent)_____

8. cat, someone in pain, coyote — _____(yowl)_____

9. peep, brief look, glance — _____(glimpse)_____

10. teeth, fist, steering wheel — _____(clench)_____

Review word: cloak (Lesson 17)

_____(Little Red Riding Hood)_____   _____(Superman)_____   _____(Dracula)_____

(Note: Answers may vary.)

Read the following selection to get the general meaning. Read it a second time, paying special attention to the words in dark type. Notice how they are used in sentences. These are Master Words. These are the words you will be working with in this lesson.

From **Arabian Nights**

"I **rebelled** against the King of the Genii," [the **genie** began]. "To punish me, he shut me up in this vase of copper and put on its leaden cover his seal, which is **enchantment** enough to prevent my coming out. Then he had the vase thrown into the sea. During the first period of my **captivity** I **vowed** that if anyone should free me before a hundred years passed, I would make him rich even after his death. But that century passed and no one freed me. In the second century I vowed I would give all the treasures in the world to my **deliverer**; but he never came.

"In the third, I promised to make him a king, to be always near him and to grant him three wishes every day; but that century passed away as the other two had and I remained in the same **plight**. At last I grew angry at being a captive for so long and vowed that if anyone would release me I would kill him and would only allow him to choose in what manner he should die. As you have freed me today, choose in what way you will die."

The fisherman was very unhappy. "What an unlucky man I am to have freed you! I **implore** you to spare my life."

"I have told you," said the genie, "that is impossible. Choose quickly; you are wasting time."

The fisherman began to **devise** a plot. "Since I must die," he said, "before I choose the manner of my death, I **conjure** you on your honor to tell me if you really were in that vase?"

"Yes, I was," answered the genie.

"I really cannot believe it," said the fisherman. "That vase could not contain one of your feet even, and how could it hold your whole body? I cannot believe it unless I see you go into the vase."

Then the genie began to change himself into smoke which, as before, spread over the sea and the shore and then, collecting itself together, began to go back into the vase slowly and evenly till there was nothing left outside. Then a voice came from the vase, which said to the fisherman, "Well, unbelieving fisherman, here I am in the vase. Do you believe me now?"

The fisherman, instead of answering, took the lid of lead and shut it down quickly on the vase.

EXERCISE 1

SELF-TEST: After reading the above selection, do the following. Look at the Master Words below. Underline the words that you think you know. Circle the words that you are less sure about. Draw a square around the words you don't recognize.

MASTER WORDS

captivity	genie
conjure	implore
deliverer	plight
devise	rebel
enchantment	vow

Read the selection on the preceding page again, this time paying special attention to the ten Master Words. In the (a) spaces provided below, write down what you think is the meaning of the word. After you have attempted a definition for each word, look up the word in a dictionary. In the (b) spaces, copy the appropriate dictionary definition.

1. **captivity** (n.)

   a. _____

   b. ___ imprisonment; bondage; confinement ___

2. **conjure** (v.)

   a. _____

   b. ___ to solemnly request, beg, or appeal to ___

3. **deliverer** (n.)

   a. _____

   b. ___ one who rescues or releases another from an unpleasant or dangerous situation; a liberator ___

4. **devise** (v.)

   a. _____

   b. ___ to think out; to plan; to scheme ___

5. **enchantment** (n.)

   a. _____

   b. ___ a magical spell or charm ___

6. **genie** (n.)

   a. _____

   b. ___ a spirit of Moslem mythology that works magic (also spelled jinni) ___

7. **implore** (v.)

   a. _____

   b. ___ to call upon, as for help; to beseech; to entreat; to beg ___

8. **plight** (n.)

   a. _____

   b. ___ a state or situation, usually bad ___

9. **rebel** (v.)

   a. _____

   b. ___ to resist or oppose authority ___

10. **vow** (v.)

   a. _____

   b. ___ to promise solemnly ___

EXERCISE 3

Use the following list of synonyms and antonyms to fill in the blanks. Some words have no antonyms. In such cases, the antonym blanks have been marked with an X.

assist	captor	imprisonment	plan	refuse	solution
beg	freedom	improvise	predicament	rescuer	spirit
beseech	grant	magic	promise	revolt	submit

	Synonyms	**Antonyms**
1. **rebel**	(revolt)	(submit)
2. **genie**	(spirit)	X
3. **enchantment**	(magic)	X
4. **captivity**	(imprisonment)	(freedom)
5. **vow**	(promise)	(refuse)
6. **deliverer**	(rescuer)	(captor)
7. **plight**	(predicament)	(solution)
8. **implore**	(beseech) (beg)	(grant) (assist)
9. **devise**	(plan)	(improvise)
10. **conjure**	(beg) (beseech)	(assist) (grant)

EXERCISE 4

Decide whether the first pair in the items below are synonyms or antonyms. Then choose the Master Word that shows a similar relation to the word(s) preceding the blank.

1. chute	:parachute	::develop	:	(devise)
2. clench	:relax	::jailer	:	(deliverer)
3. glimpse	:gawk	::obey	:	(rebel)
4. scramble	:scamper	::pledge	:	(vow)
5. yowl	:yelp	::demon	:	(genie)
6. descent	:ascent	::liberty	:	(captivity)
7. desperate	:reckless	::request	:	(implore)
8. hurtle	:crawl	::give	:	(conjure) (implore)
9. reserve	:unused	::sorcery	:	(enchantment)
10. flail	:fling	::difficulty	:	(plight)

The Master Words in this lesson are repeated below. From the Master Words, choose the appropriate word for the blank in each of the following sentences. Write the word in the numbered space provided at the right.

captivity	deliverer	enchantment	implore	rebel
conjure	devise	genie	plight	vow

1. Survival in the wilds of nature would be difficult, if not impossible, for animals that were born and raised in ...?... .

1. _____(captivity)_____

2. Carolyn ...?...(d, ed) her teammates to help her search for the contact lens that was somewhere on the locker room floor.

2. _____(implore) (conjure)_____

3. Moses is considered the ...?... of the Israelites, for he is said to have led them out of Egypt after more than 400 years of slavery.

3. _____(deliverer)_____

4. A witness in a court of law must ...?... to tell "the truth, the whole truth, and nothing but the truth."

4. _____(vow)_____

5. Ulysses faced the ...?... of having to sail his ship between the dangerous rock Scylla and the whirlpool Charybdis.

5. _____(plight)_____

6. The fairy king used a magic potion to put the humans under (a, an) ...?... .

6. _____(enchantment)_____

7. When the British Parliament passed the Stamp Act in 1765, American colonists decided to ...?... against such unfair treatment.

7. _____(rebel)_____

8. Coach Wilson tried to ...?... plays that would take the best advantage of the team's tall center and quick forwards.

8. _____(devise)_____

9. The hypnotist told his subject, "I ...?... you, tell us what past lives you have lived."

9. _____(conjure) (implore)_____

10. What would be your commands to (a, an) ...?... who would magically grant you three wishes?

10. _____(genie)_____

To complete the crossword, choose the Master Word associated with each word or phrase below. Begin each answer in the square having the same number as the clue.

1. lifesaver
2. cook up a scheme
3. state of a caged bird
4. a tight spot
5. can mean to request *or* to summon by magic
6. to plead with
7. wizards and witches have this power
8. break the rules
9. "I solemnly swear"
10. may give you three wishes

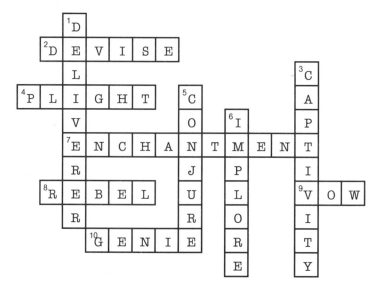

LESSON 20

Read the following selection to get the general meaning. Read it a second time, paying special attention to the words in dark type. Notice how they are used in sentences. These are Master Words. These are the words you will be working with in this lesson.

From "The Revolt of Mother"
by Mary E. Wilkins Freeman

Sarah Penn's face as she rolled her pies had that **expression** of **meek vigor** which might have **characterized** one of the New Testament saints. She was making mince pies. Her husband, Adoniram Penn, liked them better than any other kind. She baked twice a week. Adoniram often liked a piece of pie between meals. She hurried this morning. It had been later than usual when she began, and she wanted to have a pie baked for dinner. However deep a **resentment** she might be forced to hold against her husband, she would never fail in [devoted] attention to his wants.

Nobility of character **manifests** itself at **loopholes** when it is not provided with large doors. Sarah Penn's showed itself today in flaky dishes of pastry. So she made the pies faithfully, while across the table she could see, when she glanced up from her work, the sight that **rankled** in her patient and **steadfast** soul— the digging of the cellar of the new barn in the place where Adoniram forty years ago had promised her their new house should stand.

The pies were done for dinner. Adoniram and Sammy were home a few minutes after twelve o'clock. The dinner was eaten with serious haste. There was never much conversation at the table in the Penn family. Adoniram asked a blessing, and they ate promptly, then rose up and went about their work.

EXERCISE 1

SELF-TEST: After reading the above selection, do the following. Look at the Master Words below. Underline the words that you think you know. Circle the words that you are less sure about. Draw a square around the words you don't recognize.

MASTER WORDS

characterize	nobility
expression	rankle
loophole	resentment
manifest	steadfast
meek	vigor

Read the selection on the preceding page again, this time paying special attention to the ten Master Words. In the (a) spaces provided below, write down what you think is the meaning of the word. After you have attempted a definition for each word, look up the word in a dictionary. In the (b) spaces, copy the appropriate dictionary definition.

1. **characterize** (v.)

   a. _____

   b. _____ to mark or distinguish; to indicate a particular quality _____

2. **expression** (n.)

   a. _____

   b. _____ a look on the face which reveals one's feelings _____

3. **loophole** (n.)

   a. _____

   b. _____ a small opening that offers a means of defense or escape _____

4. **manifest** (v.)

   a. _____

   b. _____ to make evident or obvious; to reveal; to show _____

5. **meek** (adj.)

   a. _____

   b. _____ mild-tempered; patient; gentle _____

6. **nobility** (n.)

   a. _____

   b. _____ quality of being worthy or high in rank, mind, or character _____

7. **rankle** (v.)

   a. _____

   b. _____ to keep within the mind irritation or resentment which becomes increasingly painful _____

8. **resentment** (n.)

   a. _____

   b. _____ anger or displeasure due to an injury or insult _____

9. **steadfast** (adj.)

   a. _____

   b. _____ faithful; loyal; true; fixed or unchanging _____

10. **vigor** (n.)

   a. _____

   b. _____ mental or physical strength or energy _____

Use the following list of synonyms and antonyms to fill in the blanks. Some words have no antonyms. In such cases, the antonym blanks have been marked with an X.

anger	deadpan	gratitude	look	obstacle	reveal
baseness	disloyal	greatness	mark	opening	soothe
bother	energy	humble	misrepresent	proud	weakness
conceal	faithful				

	Synonyms	**Antonyms**
1. **expression**	(look)	(deadpan)
2. **meek**	(humble)	(proud)
3. **vigor**	(energy)	(weakness)
4. **characterize**	(mark)	(misrepresent)
5. **resentment**	(anger)	(gratitude)
6. **nobility**	(greatness)	(baseness)
7. **manifest**	(reveal)	(conceal)
8. **loophole**	(opening)	(obstacle)
9. **rankle**	(bother)	(soothe)
10. **steadfast**	(faithful)	(disloyal)

Decide whether the first pair in the items below are synonyms or antonyms. Then choose the Master Word that shows a similar relation to the word(s) preceding the blank.

1. devise	:create	::appearance	:	(expression)
2. vow	:swear	::irritate	:	(rankle)
3. deliverer	:slave driver	::unfaithful	:	(steadfast)
4. rebel	:accept	::hide	:	(manifest)
5. genie	:spirit	::dignity	:	(nobility)
6. captivity	:independence	::overbearing	:	(meek)
7. conjure	:ask	::bitterness	:	(resentment)
8. implore	:bestow	::barrier	:	(loophole)
9. enchantment	:wizardry	::distinguish	:	(characterize)
10. plight	:trouble	::strength	:	(vigor)

The Master Words in this lesson are repeated below. From the Master Words, choose the appropriate word for the blank in each of the following sentences. Write the word in the numbered space provided at the right.

| characterize | loophole | meek | rankle | steadfast |
| expression | manifest | nobility | resentment | vigor |

1. Hector felt refreshed and full of ...?... after a good night's rest.

1. ___(vigor)___

2. Janice felt ...?... growing because, although the best qualified, she was not chosen for the lead in the school play.

2. ___(resentment)___

3. Mother didn't have to ask if we had won the game; she could tell from our gloomy ...?...(s) that we had lost.

3. ___(expression)___

4. A willingness to make fools of themselves is what ...?...(s) most of the winners on that game show.

4. ___(characterize)___

5. Joe meant no harm by his careless comment, but the more I thought about it, the more it ...?...(d, ed) me.

5. ___(rankle)___

6. Although a man of humble birth, Abraham Lincoln was known for his ...?... of character.

6. ___(nobility)___

7. Even when the team made a poor showing, the Pep Club was ...?... in its support.

7. ___(steadfast)___

8. Margo had kept a cheerful attitude throughout her brother's illness, but suddenly her concern ...?...(d, ed) itself in tears.

8. ___(manifest)___

9. The lawyer could not find one ...?... in the law to save her client from going to prison.

9. ___(loophole)___

10. Walter Mitty was (a, an) ...?... man who was daring only in his romantic dreams.

10. ___(meek)___

Order the words in each item from *least* to *most.* Use the abbreviations *L* for "least" and *M* for "most." Leave the line before the word of the middle degree blank. The first word provides a clue about how to arrange the words. See the example.

sanitary: ___M___disinfected   _____scrubbed   ___L___washed
(*Washed* indicates the least sanitary; *disinfected* indicates the most sanitary.)

1. detailed: _____characterize   ___(L)___sketch   ___(M)___dissect

2. irritation: ___(M)___anger   _____resentment   ___(L)___displeasure

3. energy: _____strength   ___(M)___vigor   ___(L)___fatigue

4. worthiness: _____goodness   ___(L)___phoniness   ___(M)___nobility

5. constant: ___(M)___steadfast   ___(L)___unfaithful   _____wavering

6. annoyed: ___(M)___enrage   _____rankle   ___(L)___ruffle

7. emotional: _____expression   ___(M)___outburst   ___(L)___poker face

8. chance for freedom: ___(M)___exit   ___(L)___loophole   _____escape hatch

9. hidden: ___(L)___manifest   _____veiled   ___(M)___invisible

10. bold: ___(L)___meek   ___(M)___aggressive   _____confident

(Note: In some cases, answers may vary.)

LESSON 21

Read the following selection to get the general meaning. Read it a second time, paying special attention to the words in dark type. Notice how they are used in sentences. These are Master Words. These are the words you will be working with in this lesson.

Adapted from **The Land of Oz**
by L. Frank Baum

"It is but honest that I should **acknowledge** at the beginning of my **recital** that I was born an ordinary Woggle-Bug," began the creature, in a **frank** and friendly tone. "Knowing no better, I used my arms as well as my legs for walking, and crawled under the edges of stones or hid among the roots of grasses with no thought beyond finding a few insects smaller than myself to feed upon.

"The chill nights **rendered** me stiff and motionless, for I wore no clothing, but each morning the warm rays of the sun gave me new life and **restored** me to activity. A horrible **existence** is this, but you must remember it is the regularly **ordained** existence of Woggle-Bugs, as well as of many other tiny creatures that **inhabit** the earth.

"But **Destiny** had **singled** me out, humble though I was, for a grander fate! One day I crawled near to a country school house, and my curiosity being excited by the hum of the students within, I made bold to enter and creep along a crack between two boards until I reached the far end, where, in front of a warm fireplace, sat the master at his desk.

"No one noticed so small a creature as a Woggle-Bug, and when I found that the fireplace was even warmer and more comfortable than the sunshine, I decided to establish my future home beside it. So I found a charming nest between two bricks and hid myself therein for many, many months.

"Professor Nowitall is, doubtless, the most famous scholar in the land of Oz, and after a few days I began to listen to the lectures he gave his pupils. Not one of the pupils paid more attention than the humble, unnoticed Woggle-Bug, and I acquired in this way an amount of knowledge that is simply remarkable. That is why I place 'T.E.'—Thoroughly Educated—upon my cards."

EXERCISE 1

SELF-TEST: After reading the above selection, do the following. Look at the Master Words below. Underline the words that you think you know. Circle the words that you are less sure about. Draw a square around the words you don't recognize.

MASTER WORDS

acknowledge	ordain
destiny	recital
existence	render
frank	restore
inhabit	single

Read the selection on the preceding page again, this time paying special attention to the ten Master Words. In the (a) spaces provided below, write down what you think is the meaning of the word. After you have attempted a definition for each word, look up the word in a dictionary. In the (b) spaces, copy the appropriate dictionary definition.

1. **acknowledge** (v.)

   a. _____

   b. to recognize and accept as a fact; to admit

2. **destiny** (n.)

   a. _____

   b. the power or force said to determine the course of events

3. **existence** (n.)

   a. _____

   b. the manner of living; also, the state of being alive

4. **frank** (adj.)

   a. _____

   b. truthful and open in speech; outspoken; candid; sincere

5. **inhabit** (v.)

   a. _____

   b. to live in; to make one's home in

6. **ordain** (v.)

   a. _____

   b. to establish by law, decree, or destiny

7. **recital** (n.)

   a. _____

   b. the act of telling a story, usually to an audience

8. **render** (v.)

   a. _____

   b. to cause to be or become; to make

9. **restore** (v.)

   a. _____

   b. to return to an earlier condition; to renew

10. **single** (v.)

    a. _____

    b. (usually used with "out") to select from among a group; to set apart

Use the following list of synonyms and antonyms to fill in the blanks. Some words have no antonyms. In such cases, the antonym blanks have been marked with an X.

account	death	deny	life	overlook	secretive
admit	decay	fate	make	pick	vacate
candid	decree	free choice	occupy	renew	

	Synonyms	**Antonyms**
1. **acknowledge**	(admit)	(deny)
2. **recital**	(account)	X
3. **frank**	(candid)	(secretive)
4. **render**	(make)	X
5. **restore**	(renew)	(decay)
6. **existence**	(life)	(death)
7. **ordain**	(decree)	X
8. **inhabit**	(occupy)	(vacate)
9. **destiny**	(fate)	(free choice)
10. **single**	(pick)	(overlook)

Decide whether the first pair in the items below are synonyms or antonyms. Then choose the Master Word that shows a similar relation to the word(s) preceding the blank.

1. steadfast	:unreliable	::dishonest	: (frank)
2. expression	:manner	::cause	: (render)
3. manifest	:cover	::ruin	: (restore)
4. rankle	:annoy	::establish	: (ordain)
5. meek	:conceited	::abandon	: (inhabit)
6. resentment	:appreciation	::extinction	: (existence)
7. nobility	:decency	::choose	: (single)
8. loophole	:blockage	::ignore	: (acknowledge)
9. characterize	:describe	::telling	: (recital)
10. vigor	:power	::chance	: (destiny)

EXERCISE 5

The Master Words in this lesson are repeated below. From the Master Words, choose the appropriate word for the blank in each of the following sentences. Write the word in the numbered space provided at the right.

acknowledge	existence	inhabit	recital	restore
destiny	frank	ordain	render	single

1. Historic buildings in Williamsburg, Virginia, have been ...?...(d, ed) to appear as they did in colonial days.

1. _____ (restore)

2. Although they had won the game, the team members had to ...?... that they had not played as well as usual.

2. _____ (acknowledge)

3. Grandpa's ...?... of his part in the rescue operation grew more dramatic with each retelling.

3. _____ (recital)

4. Scouts who attended our school talent show ...?...(d, ed) out Marcia as "most promising."

4. _____ (single)

5. The last person who ...?...(d, ed) this ghost town left over seventy years ago.

5. _____ (inhabit)

6. Some people believe what their horoscopes ...?... for their lives.

6. _____ (ordain)

7. Miss Winters welcomed the students' ...?..., honest comments on how to improve her course in American literature.

7. _____ (frank)

8. Elise was ...?...(d, ed) speechless when Andrew suddenly confessed that he loved her.

8. _____ (render)

9. Some people in America have a miserable ...?... because they lack proper food, clothing, and shelter.

9. _____ (existence)

10. Do you think our lives are shaped by ...?..., or do we determine our own fates?

10. _____ (destiny)

EXERCISE 6

To complete the word spiral, choose the Master Word associated with each phrase below. Start with 1 and fill in each answer clockwise. Be careful! Each new word may overlap the previous word by one or more letters.

1. open and honest

2. what will be, will be

3. to cause or bring about

4. put into good repair

5. detailed narration of facts

6. own up to

7. call attention to

8. life and breath

9. make a rule or law

10. live in a house, for example

1.F	R	A	N	K	2.D	E	S	T
6.A	C	K	N	O	W	L	E	I
L	N	C	E	9.O	R	D	D	N
A	E					A	G	Y
T	T	T				10.I	E	3.R
I	S	I	B	A	H	N	7.S	E
C	I	X	8.E	L	G	N	I	N
E	5.R	O	T	S	E	4.R	E	D

Read the following selection to get the general meaning. Read it a second time, paying special attention to the words in dark type. Notice how they are used in sentences. These are Master Words. These are the words you will be working with in this lesson.

From **Five Little Peppers and How They Grew** by Margaret Sidney

"We never had a Christmas," said little Davie reflectively. "What are they like, Jasper?"

Jasper sat quite still, and didn't reply to this question for a moment or two.

To be among children who didn't like Thanksgiving, and who never had seen a Christmas and didn't know what it was like, was a **revelation** to him.

"They hang up stockings," said Polly softly.

How many many times she had begged her mother to try it for the younger ones; but there was never anything to put in them, and the winters were cold and hard, and only the **strictest economy** carried them through.

"Oh!" said little Phronsie in horror, "are their feet in 'em, Polly?"

"No, dear," said Polly, while Jasper, instead of laughing, only stared. Something requiring a deal of thought was passing through the boy's mind just then. "They *shall* have a Christmas!" he muttered. "I know father'll let me." But he kept his thoughts to himself; and becoming his own gay, kindly self, he explained, and told to Phronsie and the others so many stories of past Christmases he had enjoyed that the interest over the baking soon **dwindled** away, until a horrible smell of something burning brought them all to their senses.

"Oh! the house is a-burning!" cried Polly. "Oh, get a pail of water!"

" 'Tisn't either," said Jasper, snuffing wisely. "Oh! I know—I forgot all about it—I do beg your pardon." And running to the stove, he knelt down and drew out of the oven a black, odorous mass, which with a **crestfallen** air he brought to Polly.

"I'm no end sorry I made such a mess of it," he said, "I meant it for you."

" 'Tisn't any matter," said Polly kindly.

"And now do you go on," cried Joel and David, both in the same breath, "all about the Tree, you know."

"Yes, yes," said the others, "if you're not tired, Jasper."

"Oh, no," cried their **accommodating** friend, "I love to tell about it. Only wait—let's help Polly clear up first."

So after all **traces** of the **frolic** had been **tidied** up and made nice for the mother's return, they took seats in a circle, and Jasper **regaled** them with [stories and memories] till they felt as if fairyland were nothing to it!

EXERCISE 1

SELF-TEST: After reading the above selection, do the following. Look at the Master Words below. Underline the words that you think you know. Circle the words that you are less sure about. Draw a square around the words you don't recognize.

MASTER WORDS

accommodating	**frolic**	**strict**
crestfallen	**regale**	**tidy**
dwindle	**revelation**	**trace**
economy		

Read the selection on the preceding page again, this time paying special attention to the ten Master Words. In the (a) spaces provided below, write down what you think is the meaning of the word. After you have attempted a definition for each word, look up the word in a dictionary. In the (b) spaces, copy the appropriate dictionary definition.

1. **accommodating** (adj.)

   a. _____

   b. _____ eager to please; agreeable; willing to help _____

2. **crestfallen** (adj.)

   a. _____

   b. _____ dejected; depressed; downcast _____

3. **dwindle** (v.)

   a. _____

   b. _____ to become less; to fade or waste away _____

4. **economy** (n.)

   a. _____

   b. _____ careful management of money, materials, or resources so as to avoid waste _____

5. **frolic** (n.)

   a. _____

   b. _____ merrymaking; fun; carefree time _____

6. **regale** (v.)

   a. _____

   b. _____ to delight or entertain with something amusing, interesting, or pleasing _____

7. **revelation** (n.)

   a. _____

   b. _____ something which is disclosed to one who previously had no knowledge of it _____

8. **strict** (adj.)

   a. _____

   b. _____ governed by closely enforced rules; kept within narrow limits _____

9. **tidy** (v.)

   a. _____

   b. _____ to make neat or orderly _____

10. **trace** (n.)

    a. _____

    b. _____ a sign or a mark, often of something no longer present _____

Use the following list of synonyms and antonyms to fill in the blanks. Some words have no antonyms. In such cases, the antonym blanks have been marked with an X.

bore   disagreeable   evidence   lenient   neaten   secret
cheerful   disclosure   funeral   merrymaking obliging   thrift
cover-up   downcast   increase   mess   rigid   wastefulness
decrease   entertain

		Synonyms	**Antonyms**
1.	**revelation**	(disclosure)	(secret)
2.	**strict**	(rigid)	(lenient)
3.	**economy**	(thrift)	(wastefulness)
4.	**dwindle**	(decrease)	(increase)
5.	**crestfallen**	(downcast)	(cheerful)
6.	**accommodating**	(obliging)	(disagreeable)
7.	**trace**	(evidence)	(cover-up)
8.	**frolic**	(merrymaking)	(funeral)
9.	**tidy**	(neaten)	(mess)
10.	**regale**	(entertain)	(bore)

Decide whether the first pair in the items below are synonyms or antonyms. Then choose the Master Word that shows a similar relation to the word(s) preceding the blank.

1. render	:bring about	::discovery	: (revelation)
2. frank	:insincere	::work	: (frolic)
3. ordain	:declare	::disappointed	: (crestfallen)
4. restore	:destroy	::unfriendly	: (accommodating)
5. single	:select	::amuse	: (regale)
6. inhabit	:desert	::overspending	: (economy)
7. existence	:death	::clutter	: (tidy)
8. recital	:explanation	::harsh	: (strict)
9. acknowledge	:recognize	::fade	: (dwindle)
10. destiny	:fortune	::sign	: (trace)

The Master Words in this lesson are repeated below. From the Master Words, choose the appropriate word for the blank in each of the following sentences. Write the word in the numbered space provided at the right.

| accommodating | dwindle | frolic | revelation | tidy |
| crestfallen | economy | regale | strict | trace |

1. Fritz managed to save enough to take a trip to Ireland by practicing careful ...?... .

1. _____(economy)_____

2. Jenny had allowed the weeks to ...?... so that now she had only four days to complete the six-week project.

2. _____(dwindle)_____

3. Investigators could find no ...?... of the flying saucer that was supposed to have landed in the canyon.

3. _____(trace)_____

4. Guests at the feast were splendidly ...?...(d, ed) with tropical food and drink, Hawaiian music, and hula dancers.

4. _____(regale)_____

5. Dave came home ...?... after being cut from the wrestling team.

5. _____(crestfallen)_____

6. The new playground is a perfect place for the children's ...?... .

6. _____(frolic)_____

7. The maitre d' was ...?... and readily agreed to switch our order from prime rib to less expensive chuckburgers.

7. _____(accommodating)_____

8. Coach Willis had ...?... training rules, and he sometimes dismissed players who broke those rules.

8. _____(strict)_____

9. Mother suggested that if Ben would ...?... his room, he might find the record album he had misplaced.

9. _____(tidy)_____

10. The upset victory of Harry Truman as president in 1948 was (a, an) ...?... to pollsters, who had badly misjudged the number of unhappy farmers in the country.

10. _____(revelation)_____

Write the Master Word that is associated with each word group below. Then list three things that might be associated with the review word that follows.

1. autumn leaves, melting ice, setting sun

_____(dwindle)_____

2. litter, footprint, fossil

_____(trace)_____

3. confession, eye opener, inside information

_____(revelation)_____

4. maitre d', host, doorkeeper

_____(accommodating)_____

5. a dance, fun and games, a romp

_____(frolic)_____

6. losing, getting grounded, rejection

_____(crestfallen)_____

7. recycling, compact car, savings

_____(economy)_____

8. please, delight, warm someone's heart

_____(regale)_____

9. spic-and-span, shipshape, well-organized

_____(tidy)_____

10. boot camp, crash diet, Olympic training

_____(strict)_____

Review word: expression (Lesson 20)

_____(frown)_____   _____(smile)_____   _____(grimace)_____

(Note: Answers may vary.)

LESSON 23

Read the following selection to get the general meaning. Read it a second time, paying special attention to the words in dark type. Notice how they are used in sentences. These are Master Words. These are the words you will be working with in this lesson.

From **Around the World in Eighty Days**
by Jules Verne

Phileas Fogg gazed at the **tempestuous** sea, which seemed to be struggling especially to delay him, with his [**customary**] **tranquillity**. He never changed **countenance** for an instant, though a delay of twenty hours, by making him too late for the Yokohama boat, would almost **inevitably** cause the loss of the **wager**. But this man of nerve [showed] neither impatience nor **annoyance**; it seemed as if the storm were a part of his program, and had been **foreseen**. Aouda was amazed to find him as calm as he had been from the first time she saw him.

Fix did not look at the state of things in the same light. The storm greatly pleased him. His satisfaction would have been complete had the "Rangoon" been forced to retreat before the violence of wind and waves. Each delay filled him with hope, for it became more and more [likely] that Fogg would be obliged to remain some days at Hong Kong; and now the heavens themselves became his **allies**, with the gusts and **squalls**. It mattered not that they made him sea-sick—he made no account of this inconvenience . . . .

EXERCISE 1

SELF-TEST: After reading the above selection, do the following. Look at the Master Words below. Underline the words that you think you know. Circle the words that you are less sure about. Draw a square around the words you don't recognize.

MASTER WORDS

ally	inevitable
annoyance	squall
countenance	tempestuous
customary	tranquillity
foresee	wager

Read the selection on the preceding page again, this time paying special attention to the ten Master Words. In the (a) spaces provided below, write down what you think is the meaning of the word. After you have attempted a definition for each word, look up the word in a dictionary. In the (b) spaces, copy the appropriate dictionary definition.

1. **ally** (n.)

   a. _____

   b. _____ one who gives another aid or cooperation; a supportive friend or an associate

2. **annoyance** (n.)

   a. _____

   b. _____ irritation or disturbance; nuisance

3. **countenance** (n.)

   a. _____

   b. _____ the expression on the face; appearance; also, the face itself

4. **customary** (adj.)

   a. _____

   b. _____ according to the accepted way of doing things; usual; habitual

5. **foresee** (v.)

   a. _____

   b. _____ to know or see beforehand; to have a vision of a future event

6. **inevitable** (adj.)

   a. _____

   b. _____ impossible to avoid or escape; certain to happen

7. **squall** (n.)

   a. _____

   b. _____ a gust of wind, often accompanied by rain, snow, or sleet

8. **tempestuous** (adj.)

   a. _____

   b. _____ stormy; violent; blustery

9. **tranquillity** (n.)

   a. _____

   b. _____ calmness; peacefulness; quietness

10. **wager** (n.)

   a. _____

   b. _____ a bet

Use the following list of synonyms and antonyms to fill in the blanks. Some words have no antonyms. In such cases, the antonym blanks have been marked with an X.

avoidable	calm	enemy	gust	predict	stillness
bet	certain	excitement	irritation	rare	supporter
blustery	comfort	expression	peaceful	review	usual

	Synonyms	**Antonyms**
1. **tempestuous**	(blustery)	(peaceful)
2. **customary**	(usual)	(rare)
3. **tranquillity**	(stillness) (calm)	(excitement)
4. **countenance**	(expression)	X
5. **inevitable**	(certain)	(avoidable)
6. **wager**	(bet)	X
7. **annoyance**	(irritation)	(comfort)
8. **foresee**	(predict)	(review)
9. **ally**	(supporter)	(enemy)
10. **squall**	(gust)	(calm) (stillness)

Decide whether the first pair in the items below are synonyms or antonyms. Then choose the Master Word that shows a similar relation to the word(s) preceding the blank.

1. frolic	:toil	::uproar	:	(tranquillity)
2. revelation	:news	::face	:	(countenance)
3. crestfallen	:discouraged	::gamble	:	(wager)
4. accommodating	:impolite	::escapable	:	(inevitable)
5. regale	:fascinate	::stormy	:	(tempestuous)
6. economy	:extravagance	::challenger	:	(ally)
7. tidy	:dirty	::uncommon	:	(customary)
8. strict	:stern	::windstorm	:	(squall)
9. dwindle	:expand	::pleasure	:	(annoyance)
10. trace	:clue	::forecast	:	(foresee)

The Master Words in this lesson are repeated below. From the Master Words, choose the appropriate word for the blank in each of the following sentences. Write the word in the numbered space provided at the right.

| ally | countenance | foresee | squall | tranquillity |
| annoyance | customary | inevitable | tempestuous | wager |

1. A turkey dinner with all the trimmings is ...?... for many American families on Thanksgiving Day.

1. _____ (customary)

2. In spite of many differences, the United States was (a, an) ...?... of the Soviet Union in both world wars.

2. _____ (ally)

3. The sudden ...?... sent us scurrying below deck toward the dryness and security of the ship's cabin.

3. _____ (squall)

4. Phileas Fogg made a bold ...?... that he could travel around the world in eighty days.

4. _____ (wager)

5. Christopher Columbus did not ...?... that his voyage "around the world" would result in the discovery of a new continent.

5. _____ (foresee)

6. The feedback from the microphone was (a, an) ...?... to both the speaker and her audience.

6. _____ (annoyance)

7. The eye of a hurricane is a low pressure area characterized by ...?... and, often, clear skies.

7. _____ (tranquillity)

8. One look at Tom's ...?... revealed that he, too, had heard the mysterious singing in the creaky old house.

8. _____ (countenance)

9. Icy streets at rush hour made traffic jams ...?... .

9. _____ (inevitable)

10. The years surrounding the Civil War were a bloody, ...?... period in the history of the United States.

10. _____ (tempestuous)

Use at least five Master Words from this lesson to write a scene about one of the following topics. Or create a topic of your own. Write your choice on the blank. Circle the Master Words as you use them.

Possible Topics: Feuding Friends, Shopping Mall Nightmare

_____

_____

_____

_____

_____

_____

_____

(Note: Answers will vary.)

LESSON 24

PART I: From the list below, choose the appropriate word for each sentence that follows. Use each word only once. There will be two words left over.

abandon	descent	engaged	protrude	submerge
characterize	desperate	inhabit	reputation	substantial
customary	dwindle	merciless	serviceable	

1. Penguins are _____(characterize)_____ (d, ed) by short legs, webbed feet, wings which have been reduced to flippers, and a "tuxedo-like" pattern of coloring.

2. (A, An) _____(substantial)_____ breakfast might include juice, eggs, sausage, toast, and milk.

3. Snow and ice forced many travelers to _____(abandon)_____ their cars and seek shelter.

4. If you try to park that huge camper on this narrow street, it will _____(protrude)_____ into the traffic lanes.

5. When a line is busy, the operator says, "That number is _____(engaged)_____."

6. Members of some religious groups believe that true baptism takes place only if the person is _____(submerge)_____ (d, ed) in water.

7. About twenty minutes after takeoff from Kansas City, the pilot announced that we would begin our _____(descent)_____ to land in St. Louis.

8. Though Jack claimed he'd do anything to earn some money, he refused a job as a prison guard, saying he wasn't that _____(desperate)_____.

9. The importance of Wells, Fargo, and Company as a means of cross-country travel _____(dwindle)_____ (d, ed) after the Central-Union Pacific Railroad was completed in 1869.

10. Winston's _____(reputation)_____ suffered when he was falsely accused of a crime, but not his character.

11. The _____(merciless)_____ landlord told the family to leave the apartment though they had nowhere to go but the streets.

12. For adults, the _____(customary)_____ welcome to a newcomer is a handshake.

PART II: Decide whether the first pair in the items below are synonyms or antonyms. Then choose a Master Word from Lessons 13-23 which shows a similar relation to the word(s) preceding the blank. Do not repeat a Master Word that appears in the first column.

1. indefinite :measurable ::foe : _____(ally)_____

2. impractical :senseless ::saving : _____(economy)_____

3. tempestuous :calm ::surrender : _____(resistance)_____

4. bogged :tangled ::confinement : _____(captivity)_____

5. rebel :disobey ::illustrate : _____(depict)_____

(Note: Other answers may be possible.)

PART III: From the list below, choose the appropriate word for each sentence that follows. Use each word only once. There will be two words left over.

acknowledge	exhaustion	inevitable	rebel	scramble
crestfallen	foresee	instinct	render	severe
devise	frank	preserve	resentment	

1. Following passage of the Homestead Act in 1862, thousands of people _____(scramble)_____ (d, ed) westward to settle the new frontier.

2. When Tim learned that the student who sold the most magazines would win a trip, he began to _____(devise)_____ ways of attracting new customers.

3. For the president to _____(acknowledge)_____ that he had made a mistake was difficult; however, it won him the respect and support of Americans.

4. My _____(resentment)_____ of Claudia began to fade when I saw she had not meant to hurt my feelings but just give me some helpful tips.

5. Many disagreements can be solved by (a, an) _____(frank)_____ discussion in which all parties involved express their views clearly and calmly.

6. Some people wanted to combine the two clubs, but the officers believed that each club should _____(preserve)_____ its own identity.

7. The automobile _____(render)_____ (d, ed) horse-drawn vehicles obsolete.

8. The American colonists decided to _____(rebel)_____ against the laws and taxes placed on them by the British.

9. In addition to health and happiness, the palm reader declared that she could _____(foresee)_____ wealth and travel for me.

10. Growing old is _____(inevitable)_____; so are death and taxes.

11. Manda expected her punishment would be _____(severe)_____ after she dented the car, but her parents were very understanding.

12. Rhonda looks _____(crestfallen)_____—she expected to win that prize.

PART IV: Decide whether the first pair in the items below are synonyms or antonyms. Then choose a Master Word from Lessons 13-23 which shows a similar relation to the word(s) preceding the blank. Do not repeat a Master Word that appears in the first column.

1. goad   :push   ::make known   : ___(manifest)___

2. accommodating :uncooperative ::fairness   : ___(injustice)___

3. meek   :obedient   ::dedicated   : ___(steadfast)___

4. implore   :ask   ::luck   : ___(destiny)___

5. portly   :plump   ::last-mentioned : ___(latter)___

(Note: Other answers may be possible.)

Read the following selection to get the general meaning. Read it a second time, paying special attention to the words in dark type. Notice how they are used in sentences. These are Master Words. These are the words you will be working with in this lesson.

Adapted from **"A Little Cloud"** from **Dubliners** by James Joyce

Little Chandler's thoughts ever since lunchtime had been of his meeting with Gallaher, of Gallaher's invitation and of the great city London where Gallaher lived. He was called Little Chandler because, though he was but slightly under the average **stature**, he gave one the idea of being a little man. His hands were white and small, his frame was **fragile**, his voice was quiet and his manners were **refined**. He took the greatest care of his fair silken hair and moustache and used perfume **discreetly** on his handkerchief. The halfmoons of his nails were [**flawless**] and when he smiled you caught a glimpse of a row of childish white teeth.

As he sat at his desk in the King's Inns he thought what changes those eight years had brought. The friend whom he had known under a **shabby guise** had become a brilliant figure of the London Press. He turned often from his tiresome writing to gaze out of the office window. The glow of a late autumn sunset covered the grass plots and walks. It cast a shower of kindly golden dust on the untidy nurses and **decrepit** old men who **drowsed** on the benches; it **flickered** upon all the moving figures—on the children who ran screaming along the gravel paths and on everyone who passed through the gardens. He watched the scene and thought of life; and (as always happened when he thought of life) he became sad.

EXERCISE 1

SELF-TEST: After reading the above selection, do the following. Look at the Master Words below. Underline the words that you think you know. Circle the words that you are less sure about. Draw a square around the words you don't recognize.

MASTER WORDS

decrepit	fragile
discreet	guise
drowse	refined
flawless	shabby
flicker	stature

Read the selection on the preceding page again, this time paying special attention to the ten Master Words. In the (a) spaces provided below, write down what you think is the meaning of the word. After you have attempted a definition for each word, look up the word in a dictionary. In the (b) spaces, copy the appropriate dictionary definition.

1. **decrepit** (adj.)

    a. _____

    b. ___ broken down; worn out or weakened by old age ___

2. **discreet** (adj.)

    a. _____

    b. ___ showing good judgment in behavior and speech; prudent; cautious ___

3. **drowse** (v.)

    a. _____

    b. ___ to be half asleep ___

4. **flawless** (adj.)

    a. _____

    b. ___ without any imperfection; faultless; perfect ___

5. **flicker** (v.)

    a. _____

    b. ___ to shine with a wavering light; to burn unsteadily ___

6. **fragile** (adj.)

    a. _____

    b. ___ easily broken; brittle; frail ___

7. **guise** (n.)

    a. _____

    b. ___ outward appearance, often with the purpose of deceiving or masking ___

8. **refined** (adj.)

    a. _____

    b. ___ free from crudeness or vulgarity; cultured; polished ___

9. **shabby** (adj.)

    a. _____

    b. ___ appearing worn out; faded or ragged ___

10. **stature** (n.)

    a. _____

    b. ___ height of a person or animal ___

EXERCISE 3

Use the following list of synonyms and antonyms to fill in the blanks. Some words have no antonyms. In such cases, the antonym blanks have been marked with an X.

appearance	careful	faulty	height	perfect	robust
awaken	crude	feeble	imprudent	ragged	tough
beam	cultured	frail	neat	reality	waver
breadth	doze				

	Synonyms	**Antonyms**
1. **stature**	(height)	(breadth)
2. **fragile**	(frail) (feeble)	(tough) (robust)
3. **refined**	(cultured)	(crude)
4. **discreet**	(careful)	(imprudent)
5. **shabby**	(ragged)	(neat)
6. **flawless**	(perfect)	(faulty)
7. **guise**	(appearance)	(reality)
8. **decrepit**	(feeble) (frail)	(robust) (tough)
9. **drowse**	(doze)	(awaken)
10. **flicker**	(waver)	(beam)

EXERCISE 4

Decide whether the first pair in the items below are synonyms or antonyms. Then choose the Master Word that shows a similar relation to the word(s) preceding the blank.

1. tranquillity	:unrest	::strong	:	(fragile)
2. countenance	:appearance	::nap	:	(drowse)
3. inevitable	:preventable	::luxurious	:	(shabby)
4. wager	:bet	::image	:	(guise)
5. ally	:opponent	::blaze	:	(flicker)
6. customary	:exceptional	::rough	:	(refined)
7. tempestuous	:violent	::undamaged	:	(flawless)
8. squall	:gale	::size	:	(stature)
9. foresee	:foretell	::weak	:	(decrepit)
10. annoyance	:enjoyment	::careless	:	(discreet)

The Master Words in this lesson are repeated below. From the Master Words, choose the appropriate word for the blank in each of the following sentences. Write the word in the numbered space provided at the right.

| decrepit | drowse | flicker | guise | shabby |
| discreet | flawless | fragile | refined | stature |

1. Kenny is determined to play basketball, despite his small ...?... .

1. _____ (stature)

2. The large, portly woman looked strong, but when she shuffled across the room, we saw that old age had made her ...?... .

2. _____ (decrepit)

3. The young woman spoke ...?... Italian, reflecting the years of education she had received in Rome.

3. _____ (flawless)

4. A gentle breeze made the sunlight ...?... through the leaves of the maple tree.

4. _____ (flicker)

5. Grandmother showed us the ...?... vase that had been hand-painted by her mother many years ago.

5. _____ (fragile)

6. Because Alice was ...?..., Lenny knew she could be trusted not to repeat the rumor.

6. _____ (discreet)

7. What could be more relaxing than to read and ...?... in a hammock on a summer afternoon?

7. _____ (drowse)

8. Mother protested that my clothes looked ...?..., but I assured her they were merely "broken in" and comfortable.

8. _____ (shabby)

9. The suspect's ...?... of innocence clashed with the evidence which pointed to his guilt.

9. _____ (guise)

10. George is a man of ...?... taste; he prefers opera to pop music, theater to TV, and steak to hamburger.

10. _____ (refined)

To complete the crossword, choose the Master Word associated with each word or phrase below. Begin each answer in the square having the same number as the clue.

1. a perfect diamond is this

2. stamped on a box of new china

3. candle flames do this in a breeze

4. a countenance that may be a mask

5. Paul Bunyan was great in this

6. what abandoned houses soon become

7. old workhorses get this way

8. what pure sugar has been

9. not a tattletale

10. catnap

LESSON 26

Read the following selection to get the general meaning. Read it a second time, paying special attention to the words in dark type. Notice how they are used in sentences. These are Master Words. These are the words you will be working with in this lesson.

From "Li Chang's Million"
by Henry Gregor Felsen

I was positive the old **rascal** could speak excellent English. Most of the Chinese **merchants** can, but they do better business with Americans if they pretend they know no English. "It's very badly made," I said, touching the coat.

"Very well made," the Chinese insisted, slipping his hands into the sleeves of his gown. "Most excellent workmanship."

I examined the **garment** carelessly. "Very bad," I said, just for the sake of argument. "See how badly it is sewn. It would be laughed at in America."

I looked up with a **smirk** still on my lips, hoping to **discomfit** the man. But he had moved, and when I looked up, I gazed into a pair of hurt, sad eyes.

Sitting across the room, behind a counter, unnoticed by me until this moment, sat a boy who looked to be no more than six or seven years of age. While the old men had been sitting around drinking tea, he had been working—and had not stopped until I had by word and action **indicated** my low opinion of the way the coat had been sewn.

For a moment I was completely off balance. I let the coat fall from my hand, and felt a sudden rush of shame. For the boy sat on a high stool, and before him on the counter were two squares of fur that he was sewing by hand. I walked over to him. With a small needle, he was making a line of stitches as tiny and even as could be done on any machine. It was his work I had **criticized**.

"Sorry, Junior," I said lightly. "I didn't mean to run down your work."

The boy looked at me in silence. He had the most hurt expression on his face I had ever caused anyone. I looked into his inky-black eyes, and noticed there were shadows under them. I noticed how his smooth little face already showed signs of the tired, **resigned** expression it was growing into. I noticed how his head and shoulders were already bent, and how even when he rested, his back did not straighten. We stared at one another for a long minute—this child whose work I had **sneered** at and I—and then one of the men spoke to him and he bowed his head and his small fingers took up their slow, **painstaking** stitching again.

—"Li Chang's Million" by Henry Gregor Felsen. Copyright 1948 by Henry Gregor Felsen.

EXERCISE 1

SELF-TEST: After reading the above selection, do the following. Look at the Master Words below. Underline the words that you think you know. Circle the words that you are less sure about. Draw a square around the words you don't recognize.

MASTER WORDS

criticize	merchant	resigned
discomfit	painstaking	smirk
garment	rascal	sneer
indicate		

Read the selection on the preceding page again, this time paying special attention to the ten Master Words. In the (a) spaces provided below, write down what you think is the meaning of the word. After you have attempted a definition for each word, look up the word in a dictionary. In the (b) spaces, copy the appropriate dictionary definition.

1. **criticize** (v.)

   a. _____

   b. _____ to judge, especially unfavorably; to find fault with _____

2. **discomfit** (v.)

   a. _____

   b. _____ to throw into a state of confusion or embarrassment _____

3. **garment** (n.)

   a. _____

   b. _____ any article of clothing _____

4. **indicate** (v.)

   a. _____

   b. _____ to make known; to show; also, to point out _____

5. **merchant** (n.)

   a. _____

   b. _____ one who buys and sells goods for profit; a storekeeper or shopkeeper _____

6. **painstaking** (adj.)

   a. _____

   b. _____ involving great care and concentration _____

7. **rascal** (n.)

   a. _____

   b. _____ a mischievous or dishonest person _____

8. **resigned** (adj.)

   a. _____

   b. _____ showing patient acceptance of a bad, tiring, etc., situation; accepting; meek _____

9. **smirk** (n.)

   a. _____

   b. _____ a self-satisfied or gloating smile _____

10. **sneer** (v.)

   a. _____

   b. _____ to express scorn or contempt _____

EXERCISE 3

Use the following list of synonyms and antonyms to fill in the blanks. Some words have no antonyms. In such cases, the antonym blanks have been marked with an X.

accepting	condemn	embarrass	praise	saint	show
careless	customer	grin	rebellious	scoff	soothe
clothing	diligent	hide	respect	scoundrel	storekeeper

	Synonyms	**Antonyms**
1. **rascal**	(scoundrel)	(saint)
2. **merchant**	(storekeeper)	(customer)
3. **garment**	(clothing)	X
4. **smirk**	(grin)	X
5. **discomfit**	(embarrass)	(soothe)
6. **indicate**	(show)	(hide)
7. **criticize**	(condemn)	(praise)
8. **resigned**	(accepting)	(rebellious)
9. **sneer**	(scoff)	(respect)
10. **painstaking**	(diligent)	(careless)

EXERCISE 4

Decide whether the first pair in the items below are synonyms or antonyms. Then choose the Master Word that shows a similar relation to the word(s) preceding the blank.

1. drowse	:snooze	::apparel	: (garment)
2. fragile	:sturdy	::inexact	: (painstaking)
3. guise	:mask	::disturb	: (discomfit)
4. flawless	:ideal	::disapprove	: (criticize)
5. stature	:height	::smile	: (smirk)
6. decrepit	:sickly	::reveal	: (indicate)
7. shabby	:grand	::compliment	: (sneer) (smirk)
8. flicker	:glow	::resistant	: (resigned)
9. refined	:unpolished	::angel	: (rascal)
10. discreet	:hasty	::shopper	: (merchant)

The Master Words in this lesson are repeated below. From the Master Words, choose the appropriate word for the blank in each of the following sentences. Write the word in the numbered space provided at the right.

| criticize | garment | merchant | rascal | smirk |
| discomfit | indicate | painstaking | resigned | sneer |

1. Frank was ...?... to the fact that he would never be a great athlete, though he liked playing sports.

1. __(resigned)__

2. Nothing pleases that movie reviewer; she has ...?...(d, ed) every film she's written about this year.

2. __(criticize)__

3. The ...?...(s) in the shopping center hoped to attract many customers with a "Moonlight Madness" sale.

3. __(merchant)__

4. The style and color of the ...?... were not particularly flattering to Patti's slender figure and olive complexion.

4. __(garment)__

5. The official scoreboard ...?...(d, ed) that the score was still tied at the end of the first overtime.

5. __(indicate)__

6. Restringing the pearl necklace was indeed (a, an) ...?... task.

6. __(painstaking)__

7. Roger resented Karyn's attempt to ...?... him, and he told her not to put him on the spot like that again.

7. __(discomfit)__

8. Amy displayed a satisfied ...?... after she won the wager.

8. __(smirk)__

9. Rhett Butler was (a, an) ...?... who dared to do what he pleased no matter how he offended other people.

9. __(rascal)__

10. Some down-to-earth people ...?... at those who believe that space exploration is important.

10. __(sneer)__

Fill in the chart below with the Master Word that fits each set of clues. Part of speech refers to the word's usage in the lesson. Use a dictionary when necessary.

Number of Syllables	Part of Speech	Other Clues	Master Word
3	verb	confuse or upset	1. __(discomfit)__
2	adjective	like one who's given up	2. __(resigned)__
1	noun	gloating expression	3. __(smirk)__
2	noun	a coat or other type of dress	4. __(garment)__
3	adjective	"sparing no pains"	5. __(painstaking)__
2	noun	troublemaker	6. __(rascal)__
3	verb	nit-pick	7. __(criticize)__
1	verb	turn up your nose at	8. __(sneer)__
2	noun	store owner	9. __(merchant)__
3	verb	turn signals do this	10. __(indicate)__

LESSON 27

Read the following selection to get the general meaning. Read it a second time, paying special attention to the words in dark type. Notice how they are used in sentences. These are Master Words. These are the words you will be working with in this lesson.

From **"The Happy Prince"**
by Oscar Wilde

"Swallow, Swallow, little Swallow," said the Prince, "far away across the city I see a young man in a **garret**. He is leaning over a desk covered with papers, and in a **tumbler** by his side there is a bunch of **withered** violets. His hair is brown and **crisp**, and his lips are red as a **pomegranate**, and he has large and dreamy eyes. He is trying to finish a play for the Director of the Theater, but he is too cold to write any more. There is no fire in the **grate**, and hunger has made him faint."

"I will wait with you one night longer," said the Swallow, who really had a good heart. "Shall I take him another ruby?"

"Alas! I have no ruby now," said the Prince; "my eyes are all that I have left. They are made of rare sapphires, which were brought out of India a thousand years ago. **Pluck** out one of them and take it to him. He will sell it to the jeweler, and buy food and firewood, and finish his play."

"Dear Prince," said the Swallow, "I cannot do that"; and he began to weep.

"Swallow, Swallow, little Swallow," said the Prince, "do as I command you."

So the Swallow plucked out the Prince's eye, and flew away to the student's garret. It was easy enough to get in, as there was a hole in the roof. Through this he **darted**, and came into the room. The young man had his head buried in his hands, so he did not hear the **flutter** of the bird's wings, and when he looked up he found the beautiful sapphire lying on the withered violets.

"I am beginning to be **appreciated**," he cried; "this is from some great admirer. Now I can finish my play," and he looked quite happy.

EXERCISE 1

SELF-TEST: After reading the above selection, do the following. Look at the Master Words below. Underline the words that you think you know. Circle the words that you are less sure about. Draw a square around the words you don't recognize.

MASTER WORDS

appreciate	grate
crisp	pluck
dart	pomegranate
flutter	tumbler
garret	wither

Read the selection on the preceding page again, this time paying special attention to the ten Master Words. In the (a) spaces provided below, write down what you think is the meaning of the word. After you have attempted a definition for each word, look up the word in a dictionary. In the (b) spaces, copy the appropriate dictionary definition.

1. **appreciate** (v.)

   a. _____

   b. ___ to realize the value, quality, or importance of ___

2. **crisp** (adj.)

   a. _____

   b. ___ in stiff curls or ringlets; also, firm; brittle ___

3. **dart** (v.)

   a. _____

   b. ___ to move quickly; to start suddenly and move swiftly ___

4. **flutter** (n.)

   a. _____

   b. ___ a quick, flapping motion of wings, a flag, etc. ___

5. **garret** (n.)

   a. _____

   b. ___ the part of a house just under the roof; attic ___

6. **grate** (n.)

   a. _____

   b. ___ a framework of metal bars such as that used to hold fuel in a fireplace ___

7. **pluck** (v.)

   a. _____

   b. ___ to pull out or off ___

8. **pomegranate** (n.)

   a. _____

   b. ___ a thick-skinned reddish fruit about the size of an orange with many seeds ___

9. **tumbler** (n.)

   a. _____

   b. ___ a drinking glass without a handle or a stem ___

10. **wither** (v.)

   a. _____

   b. ___ to dry out or lose freshness; to shrink, fade, or decay ___

Use the following list of synonyms and antonyms to fill in the blanks. Some words have no antonyms. In such cases, the antonym blanks have been marked with an X.

attic	dash	limp	pick	shuffle
cellar	flapping	lodge	seedy fruit	thrive
criticize	glass	metal frame	shrivel	value
curly				

		Synonyms	Antonyms
1.	**garret**	(attic)	(cellar)
2.	**tumbler**	(glass)	X
3.	**wither**	(shrivel)	(thrive)
4.	**crisp**	(curly)	(limp)
5.	**pomegranate**	(seedy fruit)	X
6.	**grate**	(metal frame)	X
7.	**pluck**	(pick)	(lodge)
8.	**dart**	(dash)	(shuffle)
9.	**flutter**	(flapping)	X
10.	**appreciate**	(value)	(criticize)

Decide whether the first pair in the items below are synonyms or antonyms. Then choose the Master Word that shows a similar relation to the word(s) preceding the blank.

1. garment	:clothing	::cup	:	(tumbler)
2. discomfit	:upset	::pull	:	(pluck)
3. painstaking	:reckless	::bloom	:	(wither)
4. criticize	:attack	::grill	:	(grate)
5. sneer	:praise	::basement	:	(garret)
6. resigned	:defiant	::soft	:	(crisp)
7. smirk	:snicker	::waving	:	(flutter)
8. rascal	:hero	::drag	:	(dart)
9. merchant	:consumer	::underrate	:	(appreciate)
10. indicate	:signal	::reddish fruit	:	(pomegranate)

The Master Words in this lesson are repeated below. From the Master Words, choose the appropriate word for the blank in each of the following sentences. Write the word in the numbered space provided at the right.

| appreciate | dart | garret | pluck | tumbler |
| crisp | flutter | grate | pomegranate | wither |

1. The ...?... of the flag was barely noticeable.

   1. _____(flutter)_____

2. Markheim climbed to the ...?... at the top of the house to get a better view of the city.

   2. _____(garret)_____

3. One of the first steps in preparing a chicken is to ...?... out the feathers.

   3. _____(pluck)_____

4. In a special promotion, the restaurant advertised the gift of a 12-ounce ...?... with the purchase of a large soft drink.

   4. _____(tumbler)_____

5. The child ...?...(d, ed) into the street after the bouncing ball, giving no notice to approaching cars.

   5. _____(dart)_____

6. Janet's new permanent had made her hair too ...?... .

   6. _____(crisp)_____

7. Plants must receive the proper amount of sunlight and water if they are not to fade and ...?... .

   7. _____(wither)_____

8. Tart ...?... seeds are an attractive addition to a fruit salad.

   8. _____(pomegranate)_____

9. While riding close to the curb, John's bicycle tire caught in the ...?... that covered the storm sewer drain.

   9. _____(grate)_____

10. Most people did not accept or ...?... the composer's work because it was so different.

   10. _____(appreciate)_____

The invented words below are formed from parts of different Master Words from this lesson. Create a definition and indicate the part of speech for each word. The first one is done for you.

tumblerpluck _(n.) padded glove for removing hot items from a dishwasher_

gratepluck ([n.] a fireplace accessory used to snatch foreign objects from the fire)

withercrisp ([adj.] dry and brittle)

garretdart ([v.] to flit from roof to roof—said of birds and radio or television signals)

Now invent your own words by combining parts of the Master Words. Create a definition for each, and indicate the word's part of speech. (You may reuse any of the word parts above in new combinations.)

1. _____ _____

2. _____ _____

(Note: Answers will vary.)

Other possibilities:

crispdart   (v.) to move quickly in small circles (as would an injured fly or an excited dog tied to a stake)

withergrate   (n.) a sanitary, biodegradable grate for use in public parks

garretwither   (n.) roof dry rot caused by excessive heat and humidity

Read the following selection to get the general meaning. Read it a second time, paying special attention to the words in dark type. Notice how they are used in sentences. These are Master Words. These are the words you will be working with in this lesson.

Adapted from **The Nitty Gritty**
by Frank Bonham

When Caesar finally arrived, he got straight to work as though **perspiration** might go out of style before dark. The two of them made a big hole in the wall. Whenever a rat showed its head one of them would **snatch** up the rifle and knock it off. Resting from brickwork, they turned up some hub caps, a couple of dozen wine bottles, and two automobile generators that might have a little value. The sun sank behind the **reservoir**, and the sky darkened to the color of crankcase drainings.

Charlie found a soggy doll. Tired, he sat on the wall and looked at it. It had no hair or lashes, but its eyes were bright blue. It put him in mind of an old woman who had been beautiful and thought she still was.

"Ouch!" someone called, breaking his fantasy. Charlie came blinking back to life to see Caesar standing in the middle of the darkening lot.

"What's the matter?" Charlie called.

"I stubbed my toe on something. It looks like a chunk of bronze or iron."

"Prob'ly a safe full of money," Charlie said. He joined him, and with scraps of metal they dug it up. What Caesar had stumbled on was a long metal box, badly **corroded** but still wearing patches of black paint.

"Strongbox, maybe!" Caesar said.

"No, it's more likely a Mickey Mouse lunchbox with the original sandwich," Charlie suggested.

The box, however, was as solid as stone. They turned it over. "Hey!" Charlie exclaimed. "It's a pay phone!"

The telephone was of a very old type, the cord rotted away and the receiver a **truncated** cone that you held to your ear. He had seen telephones just like it in gangster movies.

Caesar chuckled. "Somebody must've stolen it out of a phone booth," he said. "Then he got the money out and dumped it here."

"But the lock isn't broken," Charlie pointed out. "Maybe he had to get rid of it in a hurry."

When he shook the telephone, there was a dull [**clatter**] of coins. Caesar scrambled back to the wall and got a screwdriver. By the time he returned, Charlie had broken into the money box with a piece of concrete. They spread a piece of tar paper on the ground, and in the cold, smoggy **dusk** shook out the coins. Some were **welded** together by corrosion; most of them, however, were in surprisingly good condition.

"I hardly ever saw any quarters like these," said Charlie. "They must be pretty old. I don't know how old the phone is, but it doesn't even have a dial."

They counted the money. There was nine dollars and seventy-five cents! They [**sorted**] through the coins, **squinting** at them in the dark. Nearly all the nickles had buffaloes and Indians on them, and the dimes bore a woman's head, not Mr. Roosevelt's.

—The Nitty Gritty by Frank Bonham. Copyright 1968 by Frank Bonham. E. P. Dutton and Co., Publishers.

EXERCISE 1

SELF-TEST: After reading the above selection, do the following. Look at the Master Words below. Underline the words that you think you know. Circle the words that you are less sure about. Draw a square around the words you don't recognize.

MASTER WORDS

clatter	dusk	reservoir	sort	truncated
corrode	perspiration	snatch	squint	weld

Read the selection on the preceding page again, this time paying special attention to the ten Master Words. In the (a) spaces provided below, write down what you think is the meaning of the word. After you have attempted a definition for each word, look up the word in a dictionary. In the (b) spaces, copy the appropriate dictionary definition.

1. **clatter** (n.)

   a. _____

   b. _____ a rattling noise, especially the sound made by hard objects knocking quickly together

2. **corrode** (v.)

   a. _____

   b. _____ to eat away or wear away; to decay or rust

3. **dusk** (n.)

   a. _____

   b. _____ a time between daylight and darkness in the evening

4. **perspiration** (n.)

   a. _____

   b. _____ the moisture given off through the pores of the skin; sweat

5. **reservoir** (n.)

   a. _____

   b. _____ the water supply for a large number of people; also, a place where anything is collected and stored

6. **snatch** (v.)

   a. _____

   b. _____ to grasp or seize suddenly and quickly

7. **sort** (v.)

   a. _____

   b. _____ to put in order or arrange according to kind or class; to classify

8. **squint** (v.)

   a. _____

   b. _____ to look through partly closed eyes

9. **truncated** (adj.)

   a. _____

   b. _____ cut off or shortened

10. **weld** (v.)

    a. _____

    b. _____ to join metallic parts by heating, hammering, or both; to unite things so that they become one

Use the following list of synonyms and antonyms to fill in the blanks. Some words have no antonyms. In such cases, the antonym blanks have been marked with an X.

classify	extended	polish	rust	shortened	twilight
dawn	goggle	rattle	separate	silence	unite
disorganize	grab	release	sewer	sweat	waterworks
dryness	peer				

	Synonyms	**Antonyms**
1. **perspiration**	(sweat)	(dryness)
2. **snatch**	(grab)	(release)
3. **reservoir**	(waterworks)	(sewer)
4. **corrode**	(rust)	(polish)
5. **truncated**	(shortened)	(extended)
6. **clatter**	(rattle)	(silence)
7. **dusk**	(twilight)	(dawn)
8. **weld**	(unite)	(separate)
9. **sort**	(classify)	(disorganize)
10. **squint**	(peer)	(goggle)

Decide whether the first pair in the items below are synonyms or antonyms. Then choose the Master Word that shows a similar relation to the word(s) preceding the blank.

1. wither	:flourish	::restore	: (corrode)
2. tumbler	:glass	::water supply	: (reservoir)
3. pluck	:snatch	::dampness	: (perspiration)
4. garret	:cellar	::sunrise	: (dusk)
5. grate	:fire holder	::reduced	: (truncated)
6. crisp	:soggy	::quiet	: (clatter)
7. flutter	:flurry	::organize	: (sort)
8. pomegranate	:seedy fruit	::peek	: (squint)
9. dart	:hobble	::drop	: (snatch)
10. appreciate	:insult	::detach	: (weld)

LESSON TWENTY-EIGHT

EXERCISE 5

The Master Words in this lesson are repeated below. From the Master Words, choose the appropriate word for the blank in each of the following sentences. Write the word in the numbered space provided at the right.

| clatter | dusk | reservoir | sort | truncated |
| corrode | perspiration | snatch | squint | weld |

1. The saleswoman guaranteed that the metal on my car would not ...?... if I had it rust-proofed.

1. _____ (corrode)

2. ...?... glistened on the shoulders of the basketball players as they stumbled toward the locker room after a tough game.

2. _____ (Perspiration)

3. Lake Mead, the ...?... behind Hoover Dam, supplies water to most of Arizona, Nevada, and southern California.

3. _____ (reservoir)

4. Many post offices employ machines that can "read" ZIP codes; thus, mail can be ...?...(d, ed) mechanically.

4. _____ (sort)

5. In the cafeteria, the ...?... of dishes often interrupts conversation.

5. _____ (clatter)

6. When we came out of the cave, we ...?...(d, ed) until our eyes adjusted to the bright sunlight.

6. _____ (squint)

7. All the divers complained about the new, ...?... board, and they wanted the old, longer board back.

7. _____ (truncated)

8. The Constitution ...?...(d, ed) the thirteen colonies into the United States of America.

8. _____ (weld)

9. The squirrel ...?...(d, ed) up acorns to store away for winter.

9. _____ (snatch)

10. You can begin looking for fireflies to appear after ...?... falls.

10. _____ (dusk)

EXERCISE 6

To complete this puzzle, fill in the Master Word associated with each phrase below. Then unscramble the circled letters to form a Master Word from Lesson 27, and define it.

1. often a sign of hard work — (p) e r s (p) i r a t i o n
2. pencils falling on the floor would do this — (c) l (a) t t e r
3. melt two pieces into one — w (e) l d
4. the trunk of a chopped tree is this — (t) r u n c a t e d
5. a shoplifter may do this — s n (a) t c h
6. stainless steel won't do this — c o (r) r o d e
7. what a bank teller does with money — s o r t
8. could be the site of a dam — r e s (e) r v o i r
9. vampire's wake-up time — d u s k
10. bright light may make you do this — s q u (i) n t

Unscrambled word: _____ (appreciate)

Definition: _____ (to realize the value, quality, or importance of)

(Note: Definition may vary.)

Read the following selection to get the general meaning. Read it a second time, paying special attention to the words in dark type. Notice how they are used in sentences. These are Master Words. These are the words you will be working with in this lesson.

From **The Red Pony**
by John Steinbeck

"That's old Easter," Jody explained. "That's the first horse my father ever had. He's thirty years old." He looked up into Gitano's old eyes for some **response**.

"No good any more," Gitano said.

Jody's father and Billy Buck came out of the barn and walked over.

"Too old to work," Gitano repeated. "Just eats and pretty soon dies."

Carl Tiflin caught the last words. He hated his **brutality** toward old Gitano, and so he became brutal again.

"It's a shame not to shoot Easter," he said. "It'd save him a lot of pains and rheumatism." He looked secretly at Gitano, to see whether he noticed the **parallel**, but the big bony hands did not move, nor did the dark eyes turn from the horse. "Old things ought to be put out of their **misery**," Jody's father went on. "One shot, a big noise, one big pain in the head maybe, and that's all. That's better than stiffness and sore teeth."

Billy Buck broke in. "They got a right to rest after they worked all of their life. Maybe they like to just walk around."

Carl had been looking **steadily** at the skinny horse. "You can't imagine now what Easter used to look like," he said softly. "High neck, deep chest, fine barrel. He could jump a five-bar gate in stride. I won a flat race on him when I was fifteen years old. I could of got two hundred dollars for him any time. You wouldn' think how pretty he was." He **checked** himself, for he hated softness. "But he ought to be shot now," he said.

"He's got a right to rest," Billy Buck insisted.

Jody's father had a **humorous** thought. He turned to Gitano. "If ham and eggs grew on a side-hill I'd turn you out to pasture too," he said. "But I can't **afford** to pasture you in my kitchen."

He laughed to Billy Buck about it as they went on toward the house. "Be a good thing for all of us if ham and eggs grew on the side-hills."

Jody knew how his father was **probing** for a place to hurt Gitano. He had been probed often. His father knew every place in the boy where a word would **fester**.

EXERCISE 1

SELF-TEST: After reading the above selection, do the following. Look at the Master Words below. Underline the words that you think you know. Circle the words that you are less sure about. Draw a square around the words you don't recognize.

MASTER WORDS

afford	misery
brutality	parallel
check	probe
fester	response
humorous	steadily

Read the selection on the preceding page again, this time paying special attention to the ten Master Words. In the (a) spaces provided below, write down what you think is the meaning of the word. After you have attempted a definition for each word, look up the word in a dictionary. In the (b) spaces, copy the appropriate dictionary definition.

1. **afford** (v.)

    a. _____

    b. _____ to bear an expense; also, to spare _____

2. **brutality** (n.)

    a. _____

    b. _____ the state of being savage, inhuman, or cruel; also, the state of being crude, coarse, or harsh

3. **check** (v.)

    a. _____

    b. _____ to stop suddenly; to hold back or restrain _____

4. **fester** (v.)

    a. _____

    b. _____ to become painful; to rankle _____

5. **humorous** (adj.)

    a. _____

    b. _____ funny; comical; amusing _____

6. **misery** (n.)

    a. _____

    b. _____ great suffering, pain, or unhappiness; wretchedness _____

7. **parallel** (n.)

    a. _____

    b. _____ a similarity or resemblance; also a comparison _____

8. **probe** (v.)

    a. _____

    b. _____ to examine thoroughly; to search; to investigate _____

9. **response** (n.)

    a. _____

    b. _____ an answer or a reply; reaction _____

10. **steadily** (adv.)

    a. _____

    b. _____ without wavering; without interruption; constantly _____

Use the following list of synonyms and antonyms to fill in the blanks. Some words have no antonyms. In such cases, the antonym blanks have been marked with an X.

bankrupt   constantly   funny   occasionally   reaction   soothe
bear   cover up   investigate propel   serious   stimulus
bliss   cruelty   kindness   rankle   similarity   suffering
brake   difference

	Synonyms	**Antonyms**
1. **response**	(reaction)	(stimulus)
2. **brutality**	(cruelty)	(kindness)
3. **parallel**	(similarity)	(difference)
4. **misery**	(suffering)	(bliss)
5. **steadily**	(constantly)	(occasionally)
6. **check**	(brake)	(propel)
7. **humorous**	(funny)	(serious)
8. **afford**	(bear)	(bankrupt)
9. **probe**	(investigate)	(cover up)
10. **fester**	(rankle)	(soothe)

Decide whether the first pair in the items below are synonyms or antonyms. Then choose the Master Word that shows a similar relation to the word(s) preceding the blank.

1. reservoir	:tank	::annoy	: (fester)
2. perspiration	:sweat	::search	: (probe)
3. corrode	:refinish	::gentleness	: (brutality)
4. truncated	:cropped	::support	: (afford)
5. dusk	:daybreak	::continue	: (check)
6. clatter	:stillness	::irregularly	: (steadily)
7. sort	:arrange	::reply	: (response)
8. squint	:peek	::resemblance	: (parallel)
9. snatch	:throw	::happiness	: (misery)
10. weld	:split	::grim	: (humorous)

The Master Words in this lesson are repeated below. From the Master Words, choose the appropriate word for the blank in each of the following sentences. Write the word in the numbered space provided at the right.

| afford | check | humorous | parallel | response |
| brutality | fester | misery | probe | steadily |

1. In ...?... to news of the flood, thousands of people sent clothing, food, and money to aid the victims.

1. _____ (response)

2. The lawyer ...?...(d, ed) each testimony for possible lies.

2. _____ (probe)

3. Credit cards encourage many people to buy more than they can really ...?... .

3. _____ (afford)

4. The rain has fallen ...?... for three hours, so there is no doubt that the baseball game will be postponed.

4. _____ (steadily)

5. The counselor told Lauren that she must express her anger and not allow bitterness to ...?... .

5. _____ (fester)

6. Bob drew (a, an) ...?... between the national debt and his own.

6. _____ (parallel)

7. The police officer was charged with ...?... after doctors noted the thief's bruises.

7. _____ (brutality)

8. From his pedestal the Happy Prince could see all the unhappiness and ...?... of wretched people in his city.

8. _____ (misery)

9. A situation or a joke is often ...?... because we are surprised by an unexpected turn of events.

9. _____ (humorous)

10. The golfer ...?...(d, ed) her swing when she spotted someone directly ahead of her on the course.

10. _____ (check)

To complete the crossword, choose the Master Word associated with each word or phrase below. Begin each answer in the square having the same number as the clue.

1. it's said to love company
2. to get information, you could do this
3. how to walk a tightrope
4. without money or time, you can't do this
5. a wound or anger might do this
6. what jokes are meant to be
7. inhuman treatment
8. hold back
9. an analogy
10. most questions deserve one

Read the following selection to get the general meaning. Read it a second time, paying special attention to the words in dark type. Notice how they are used in sentences. These are Master Words. These are the words you will be working with in this lesson.

From **"The Legend of Sleepy Hollow"**
by Washington Irving

The **sequestered** situation of this church seems always to have made it a favorite **haunt** of troubled spirits. It stands on a **knoll**, surrounded by locust trees and [majestic] elms, from among which its **decent** whitewashed walls shine **modestly** forth, like Christian purity beaming through the shades of **retirement**. A gentle slope descended from it to a silver sheet of water, bordered by high trees, between which peeps may be caught at the blue hills of the Hudson. To look upon its grass-grown yard, where the sunbeams seem to sleep so quietly, one would think that there at least the dead might rest in peace. On one side of the church extends a wide woody **dell**, along which **raves** a large brook among broken rocks and trunks of fallen trees. Over a deep black part of the stream, not far from the church, was formerly thrown a wooden bridge; the road that led to it, and the bridge itself, were thickly shaded by overhanging trees, which cast a **gloom** about it, even in the daytime; but occasioned a fearful darkness at night. This was one of the favorite haunts of the headless horseman, and the place where he was most frequently **encountered**.

EXERCISE 1

SELF-TEST: After reading the above selection, do the following. Look at the Master Words below. Underline the words that you think you know. Circle the words that you are less sure about. Draw a square around the words you don't recognize.

MASTER WORDS

decent	knoll
dell	modest
encounter	rave
gloom	retirement
haunt	sequestered

Read the selection on the preceding page again, this time paying special attention to the ten Master Words. In the (a) spaces provided below, write down what you think is the meaning of the word. After you have attempted a definition for each word, look up the word in a dictionary. In the (b) spaces, copy the appropriate dictionary definition.

1. **decent** (adj.)

    a. _____

    b. _____ fitting; suitable; proper; appropriate

2. **dell** (n.)

    a. _____

    b. _____ a small valley

3. **encounter** (v.)

    a. _____

    b. _____ to meet, especially unexpectedly; often, to meet in opposition

4. **gloom** (n.)

    a. _____

    b. _____ darkness; dusk; also, low spirits; depression, sadness

5. **haunt** (n.)

    a. _____

    b. _____ a place frequently visited

6. **knoll** (n.)

    a. _____

    b. _____ a little rounded hill; a mound

7. **modest** (adj.)

    a. _____

    b. _____ humble; not showy or boastful

8. **rave** (v.)

    a. _____

    b. _____ to make a wild or furious sound; to storm or rage

9. **retirement** (n.)

    a. _____

    b. _____ withdrawal from society, from business, etc.; seclusion; privacy

10. **sequestered** (adj.)

    a. _____

    b. _____ set apart; secluded; isolated

Use the following list of synonyms and antonyms to fill in the blanks. Some words have no antonyms. In such cases, the antonym blanks have been marked with an X.

avoid	hill	light	murmur	roar	surrounded
connection	humble	meet	proper	seclusion	unsuitable
darkness	isolated	mound	proud	sinkhole	valley
hangout					

	Synonyms	**Antonyms**
1. **sequestered**	(isolated)	(surrounded)
2. **haunt**	(hangout)	X
3. **knoll**	(mound) (hill)	(sinkhole) (valley)
4. **decent**	(proper)	(unsuitable)
5. **modest**	(humble)	(proud)
6. **retirement**	(seclusion)	(connection)
7. **dell**	(valley) (sinkhole)	(hill) (mound)
8. **rave**	(roar)	(murmur)
9. **gloom**	(darkness)	(light)
10. **encounter**	(meet)	(avoid)

Decide whether the first pair in the items below are synonyms or antonyms. Then choose the Master Word that shows a similar relation to the word(s) preceding the blank.

1. brutality	:tenderness	::interaction	:	(retirement)
2. check	:urge	::improper	:	(decent)
3. fester	:irritate	::confront	:	(encounter)
4. steadily	:periodically	::mutter	:	(rave)
5. probe	:explore	::simple	:	(modest)
6. afford	:provide	::separated	:	(sequestered)
7. response	:feedback	::retreat	:	(haunt)
8. misery	:pleasure	::brightness	:	(gloom)
9. humorous	:comical	::lowlands	:	(dell)
10. parallel	:comparison	::hill	:	(knoll)

The Master Words in this lesson are repeated below. From the Master Words, choose the appropriate word for the blank in each of the following sentences. Write the word in the numbered space provided at the right.

| decent | encounter | haunt | modest | retirement |
| dell | gloom | knoll | rave | sequestered |

1. We decided to camp on top of the ...?... instead of in the valley in case it rained.

1. _____ (knoll)

2. United States soldiers frequently ...?...(d, ed) Viet Cong along the DMZ during the Vietnam War.

2. _____ (encounter)

3. The storm ...?...(d, ed) around us as we huddled in our stalled car.

3. _____ (rave)

4. A cloud of ...?... hung over the nation until word came that the hostages had been freed.

4. _____ (gloom)

5. I wanted to get back to nature, so I chose to vacation in (a, an) ...?... cabin in the mountains.

5. _____ (sequestered)

6. Frankie didn't see the small house hidden away in the ...?... until he reached the top of the hill.

6. _____ (dell)

7. Although the star announced that he was going into ...?..., everyone was sure he would perform again soon.

7. _____ (retirement)

8. The Peppers' home was ...?... and simple, but it was comfortable.

8. _____ (modest)

9. The King's Arms Tavern in Williamsburg, Virginia, was a favorite ...?... of important colonial thinkers.

9. _____ (haunt)

10. The Victorians did not think it was ...?... to refer to a "breast" of chicken or a table "leg."

10. _____ (decent)

To complete the word spiral, choose the Master Word associated with each phrase below. Start with 1 and fill in each answer clockwise. Be careful! Each new word may overlap the previous word by one or more letters.

1. prisoners live this kind of life

2. in good taste

3. hideaway or "stomping ground"

4. raise a ruckus

5. to "run into" someone or something

6. privacy or seclusion

7. a dune might be called this

8. dimness or murkiness

9. not extravagant or showy

10. where the farmer lives

1. S	E	Q	U	E	S	T	E
O	U	N	T	E	6. R	E	R
C	8. G	L	O	O	9. M	T	E
N	L	L	L		O	I	2. D
5. E	L	E			D	R	E
V	O	10. D	T	S	E	E	C
A	N	7. K	T	N	E	M	E
4. R	T	N	U	A	3. H	T	N

Read the following selection to get the general meaning. Read it a second time, paying special attention to the words in dark type. Notice how they are used in sentences. These are Master Words. These are the words you will be working with in this lesson.

From **Five Little Peppers and How They Grew** by Margaret Sidney

And then the carriage turned in at a brownstone gateway, and winding up among some fine old trees, stopped before a large, **stately residence** that in Polly's eye seemed like one of the castles of Ben's famous stories. And then Mr. King got out, and [proudly led] Polly out, and up the steps, while Jasper followed with Polly's bag, which he couldn't be **persuaded** to resign to Thomas. A stiff butler held the door open—and then, the rest was only a pleasant, confused **jumble** of kind welcoming words, smiling faces, with a background of high **spacious** walls, bright pictures, and soft, **elegant** hangings, everything and all **inextricably** mixed—till Polly herself seemed floating—away—away, fast to the Fairyland of her dreams. Now, Mr. King was handing her around, like a precious **parcel**, from one to the other—now Jasper was **bobbing** in and out everywhere, introducing her on all sides, and then Prince was jumping up and trying to lick her face every minute—but it was best of all when a lovely face looked down into hers and Jasper's sister bent to kiss her.

"I am *very* glad to have you here, little Polly." The words were simple, but Polly, lifting up her clear brown eyes, looked straight into the heart of the speaker, and from that moment never **ceased** to love her.

EXERCISE 1

SELF-TEST: After reading the above selection, do the following. Look at the Master Words below. Underline the words that you think you know. Circle the words that you are less sure about. Draw a square around the words you don't recognize.

MASTER WORDS

bob	**parcel**
cease	**persuade**
elegant	**residence**
inextricable	**spacious**
jumble	**stately**

Read the selection on the preceding page again, this time paying special attention to the ten Master Words. In the (a) spaces provided below, write down what you think is the meaning of the word. After you have attempted a definition for each word, look up the word in a dictionary. In the (b) spaces, copy the appropriate dictionary definition.

1. **bob** (v.)

   a. _____

   b. _____ to move up and down with short jerks _____

2. **cease** (v.)

   a. _____

   b. _____ to come to an end; to discontinue; to stop _____

3. **elegant** (adj.)

   a. _____

   b. _____ showing richness, refinement, and good taste _____

4. **inextricable** (adj.)

   a. _____

   b. _____ hopelessly tangled, complicated, or confused _____

5. **jumble** (n.)

   a. _____

   b. _____ a confused mixture; mess; disorder _____

6. **parcel** (n.)

   a. _____

   b. _____ a package or bundle _____

7. **persuade** (v.)

   a. _____

   b. _____ to convince one to act or believe in a certain way _____

8. **residence** (n.)

   a. _____

   b. _____ the place where one lives; dwelling place; home, especially a large house _____

9. **spacious** (adj.)

   a. _____

   b. _____ having much space; roomy _____

10. **stately** (adj.)

   a. _____

   b. _____ having a grand or majestic appearance; dignified; magnificent _____

EXERCISE 3

Use the following list of synonyms and antonyms to fill in the blanks. Some words have no antonyms. In such cases, the antonym blanks have been marked with an X.

arrangement   convince   discourage   glide   lowly   refined
begin   cramped   disengaged   home   majestic roomy
business   crude   entangled   jerk   package   stop
confusion

	Synonyms	**Antonyms**
1. **stately**	(majestic) (refined)	(lowly) (crude)
2. **residence**	(home)	(business)
3. **persuade**	(convince)	(discourage)
4. **jumble**	(confusion)	(arrangement)
5. **spacious**	(roomy)	(cramped)
6. **elegant**	(refined) (majestic)	(crude) (lowly)
7. **inextricable**	(entangled)	(disengaged)
8. **parcel**	(package)	X
9. **bob**	(jerk)	(glide)
10. **cease**	(stop)	(begin)

EXERCISE 4

Decide whether the first pair in the items below are synonyms or antonyms. Then choose the Master Word that shows a similar relation to the word(s) preceding the blank.

1. encounter	:face	::coax	: (persuade)
2. modest	:plain	::dwelling	: (residence)
3. retirement	:socializing	::humble	: (stately)
4. decent	:unfitting	::order	: (jumble)
5. sequestered	:secluded	::bundle	: (parcel)
6. rave	:mumble	::unrefined	: (elegant)
7. haunt	:hangout	::snarled	: (inextricable)
8. knoll	:rise	::big	: (spacious)
9. gloom	:sunniness	::slide	: (bob)
10. dell	:highland	::start	: (cease)

The Master Words in this lesson are repeated below. From the Master Words, choose the appropriate word for the blank in each of the following sentences. Write the word in the numbered space provided at the right.

bob	elegant	jumble	persuade	spacious
cease	inextricable	parcel	residence	stately

1. The strutting peacock, with his magnificent tail, is among the most ...?... members of the animal kingdom.

1. ___(stately) (elegant)___

2. As soon as the child realized that no one was going to pay attention to her fussing, she ...?...(d, ed) whining.

2. ___(cease)___

3. The pioneers eagerly awaited the Wells Fargo wagon for delivery of (a, an) ...?... .

3. ___(parcel)___

4. The maze Daedalus designed to house the Minotaur was so ...?... that the architect himself could not find his way out.

4. ___(inextricable)___

5. The Vatican is the official ...?... of the Pope.

5. ___(residence)___

6. The three boys gave their recitals of the adventure at the same time in (a, an) ...?... of excitement.

6. ___(jumble)___

7. Beginning swimmers are taught to ...?... in and out of the water in order to form the habit of rhythmic breathing.

7. ___(bob)___

8. Although Sally had many good suggestions, no one could ...?... her to run for student council president.

8. ___(persuade)___

9. The new station wagon seemed ...?... to the family after being crammed in a compact car for so many years.

9. ___(spacious)___

10. The house itself is modest, but the furnishings are ...?... .

10. ___(elegant) (stately)___

Order the words in each item from *least* to *most*. Use the abbreviations *L* for "least" and *M* for "most." Leave the line before the word of the middle degree blank. The first word provides a clue about how to arrange the words. See the example.

enthusiastic: ____inspired __L__hopeful __M__aggressive

(*Hopeful* indicates the least enthusiastic; *aggressive* indicates the most enthusiastic.)

1. roomy: ____enormous __(M)__infinite __(L)__spacious

2. sorted: ____assortment __(M)__organization __(L)__jumble

3. influencing: ____persuade __(L)__advise __(M)__brainwash

4. luxurious: ____tasteful __(L)__plain __(M)__elegant

5. bulky: ____letter __(L)__postcard __(M)__parcel

6. trapped: __(M)__inextricable ____troublesome __(L)__escapable

7. smooth: ____bob __(M)__skate __(L)__tumble

8. permanent: __(M)__residence ____dorm __(L)__hotel

9. fancy: __(M)__stately __(L)__crude ____modest

10. active: ____slow __(M)__race __(L)__cease

(Note: In some cases, answers may vary.)

Read the following selection to get the general meaning. Read it a second time, paying special attention to the words in dark type. Notice how they are used in sentences. These are Master Words. These are the words you will be working with in this lesson.

From **The Old Man and the Sea**
by Ernest Hemingway

Sometimes someone would speak in a boat. But most of the boats were silent except for the dip of the oars. They spread apart after they were out of the mouth of the **harbor** and each one headed for the part of the ocean where he hoped to find fish. The old man knew he was going far out and he left the smell of the land behind and rowed out into the clean early morning smell of the ocean. He saw the **phosphorescence** of the Gulfweed in the water as he rowed over the part of the ocean that the fishermen called the great well because there was a sudden deep of seven hundred fathoms where all sorts of fish **congregated** because of the **swirl** the current made against the steep walls of the floor of the ocean. Here there were **concentrations** of shrimp and bait fish and sometimes schools of squid in the deepest holes and these rose close to the **surface** at night where all the wandering fish fed on them.

In the dark the old man could feel the morning coming and as he rowed he heard the **trembling** sound as flying fish left the water and the hissing that their stiff set wings made as they **soared** away in the darkness. He was very fond of flying fish as they were his **principal** friends on the ocean. He was sorry for the birds, especially the small **delicate** dark terns that were always flying and looking and almost never finding, and he thought, the birds have a harder life than we do except for the robber birds and the heavy strong ones. Why did they make birds so delicate and fine as those sea swallows when the ocean can be so cruel? She is kind and very beautiful. But she can be so cruel and it comes so suddenly and such birds that fly, dipping and hunting, with their small sad voices are made too delicately for the sea.

—Copyright 1952 by Ernest Hemingway. Published by Charles Scribner's Sons, New York.

EXERCISE 1

SELF-TEST: After reading the above selection, do the following. Look at the Master Words below. Underline the words that you think you know. Circle the words that you are less sure about. Draw a square around the words you don't recognize.

MASTER WORDS

concentration	principal
congregate	soar
delicate	surface
harbor	swirl
phosphorescence	tremble

Read the selection on the preceding page again, this time paying special attention to the ten Master Words. In the (a) spaces provided below, write down what you think is the meaning of the word. After you have attempted a definition for each word, look up the word in a dictionary. In the (b) spaces, copy the appropriate dictionary definition.

1. **concentration** (n.)

   a. _____

   b. ___ state of being gathered around a common center _____

2. **congregate** (v.)

   a. _____

   b. ___ to assemble; to come together in a crowd or mass _____

3. **delicate** (adj.)

   a. _____

   b. ___ easily damaged or injured; fragile _____

4. **harbor** (n.)

   a. _____

   b. ___ part of a body of water near the shore that offers ships protection from wind and waves; hence, any refuge _____

5. **phosphorescence** (n.)

   a. _____

   b. ___ the giving off of light without heat; light generated from living organisms _____

6. **principal** (adj.)

   a. _____

   b. ___ highest in rank or importance; foremost; chief; main _____

7. **soar** (v.)

   a. _____

   b. ___ to fly upward; to rise or ascend _____

8. **surface** (n.)

   a. _____

   b. ___ the outside of a thing; the top of a body of water _____

9. **swirl** (n.)

   a. _____

   b. ___ a whirling or twisting motion _____

10. **tremble** (v.)

    a. _____

    b. ___ to shake, shiver, or quiver _____

Use the following list of synonyms and antonyms to fill in the blanks. Some words have no antonyms. In such cases, the antonym blanks have been marked with an X.

be still	exterior	hardy	least	rise	spread
chief	fragile	haven	mass	scatter	swoop
collect	glow	interior	open sea	shake	whirl
darkness					

	Synonyms	**Antonyms**
1. **harbor**	(haven)	(open sea)
2. **phosphorescence**	(glow)	(darkness)
3. **congregate**	(collect)	(scatter)
4. **swirl**	(whirl)	X
5. **concentration**	(mass)	(spread)
6. **surface**	(exterior)	(interior)
7. **tremble**	(shake)	(be still)
8. **soar**	(rise)	(swoop)
9. **principal**	(chief)	(least)
10. **delicate**	(fragile)	(hardy)

Decide whether the first pair in the items below are synonyms or antonyms. Then choose the Master Word that shows a similar relation to the word(s) preceding the blank.

1. persuade	:convert	::top	: (surface)
2. residence	:house	::shimmer	: (phosphorescence)
3. parcel	:packet	::port	: (harbor)
4. stately	:grand	::collection	: (concentration)
5. inextricable	:freed	::dip	: (soar)
6. spacious	:sizable	::spinning	: (swirl)
7. jumble	:system	::sturdy	: (delicate)
8. elegant	:coarse	::minor	: (principal)
9. bob	:bounce	::quiver	: (tremble)
10. cease	:commence	::disband	: (congregate)

The Master Words in this lesson are repeated below. From the Master Words, choose the appropriate word for the blank in each of the following sentences. Write the word in the numbered space provided at the right.

concentration	delicate	phosphorescence	soar	swirl
congregate	harbor	principal	surface	tremble

1. After we sanded and refinished the desk, its ...?... shone like new.

1. _____ (surface)

2. Hundreds of ants ...?...(d, ed) around the few drops of lemonade that had been spilled on the patio.

2. _____ (congregate)

3. Max put away the ...?... glassware and got out the plastic tumblers when his little grandson came to visit.

3. _____ (delicate)

4. A tiny ...?... of smoke in the distance indicated to the forest rangers that they had a fire to fight.

4. _____ (swirl)

5. The ...?... was a welcome sight to the Pilgrims who had crossed the Atlantic on the *Mayflower*.

5. _____ (harbor)

6. The hot air balloon ...?...(d, ed) over the city.

6. _____ (soar)

7. Does ...?... cause the fireflies to glow in the dark?

7. _____ (phosphorescence)

8. Steve's voice ...?...(d, ed) as he told about his narrow escape from the grizzly bear.

8. _____ (tremble)

9. The automobile is the ...?... means of private transportation in the United States.

9. _____ (principal)

10. Texas has a considerable ...?... of people in Dallas and Houston.

10. _____ (concentration)

Write the Master Word that is associated with each word group below. Then list three things that might be associated with the review word that follows.

1. sandpaper, table top, soap suds _____ (surface)

2. cold, earthquake, fear _____ (tremble)

3. shore, sailors, safety _____ (harbor)

4. hurricane, whirlpool, cotton candy _____ (swirl)

5. porcelain, silk, snowflakes _____ (delicate)

6. eagle, balloon, jet _____ (soar)

7. ship's captain, president, leading actor _____ (principal)

8. neon, glowworm, fireflies _____ (phosphorescence)

9. mother lode, crowd, black hole _____ (concentration)

10. concert hall, sports stadium, church _____ (congregate)

Review word: elegant (Lesson 31)

_____ (wedding)   _____ (coronation)   _____ (prom)

(Note: Answers may vary.)

Read the following selection to get the general meaning. Read it a second time, paying special attention to the words in dark type. Notice how they are used in sentences. These are Master Words. These are the words you will be working with in this lesson.

Adapted from **"The Luck of Roaring Camp"** by Bret Harte

Almost **imperceptibly** a change came over Roaring Camp. The cabin assigned to "Tommy Luck"—or "The Luck," as he was more frequently called—first showed signs of improvement. It was kept **scrupulously** clean and whitewashed. Then it was boarded, clothed, and papered. The rosewood cradle, packed eighty miles by mule, had, in Stumpy's way of putting it, "sorter killed the rest of the furniture." So the [**renovation**] of the cabin became a necessity. The men who were in the habit of **lounging** in at Stumpy's to see "how 'The Luck' got on" seemed to appreciate the change, and in self-defense the **rival establishment** of "Tuttle's Grocery"

imported a carpet and mirrors. The reflections of the latter on the appearance of Roaring Camp **tended** to produce stricter habits of personal cleanliness. Stumpy placed a kind of **quarantine** upon those who sought the honor and privilege of holding The Luck. It was cruelly shameful to Kentuck—who, in the carelessness of a large nature and the habits of frontier life, had begun to regard all garments as a second cuticle, which, like a snake's, only **sloughed** off through decay—to be denied this privilege for obvious reasons. Yet he thereafter appeared regularly every afternoon in a clean shirt with his face shining.

EXERCISE 1

SELF-TEST: After reading the above selection, do the following. Look at the Master Words below. Underline the words that you think you know. Circle the words that you are less sure about. Draw a square around the words you don't recognize.

MASTER WORDS

establishment	renovation
imperceptible	rival
import	scrupulous
lounge	slough
quarantine	tend

Read the selection on the preceding page again, this time paying special attention to the ten Master Words. In the (a) spaces provided below, write down what you think is the meaning of the word. After you have attempted a definition for each word, look up the word in a dictionary. In the (b) spaces, copy the appropriate dictionary definition.

1. **establishment** (n.)

   a. _____

   b. _____ that which is firmly fixed, such as a government, legal code, institution, or business

2. **imperceptible** (adj.)

   a. _____

   b. _____ so slight or gradual as to escape notice

3. **import** (v.)

   a. _____

   b. _____ to bring in from a foreign country or from an outside area

4. **lounge** (v.)

   a. _____

   b. _____ to pass time lazily; to loaf

5. **quarantine** (n.)

   a. _____

   b. _____ isolation imposed in order to prevent the spread of disease

6. **renovation** (n.)

   a. _____

   b. _____ a project to make something like new again; an effort to return to original condition

7. **rival** (adj.)

   a. _____

   b. _____ striving to equal or surpass; competing

8. **scrupulous** (adj.)

   a. _____

   b. _____ extremely careful in attention to details; exact; precise

9. **slough** (v.)

   a. _____

   b. _____ to shed or cast off; to discard

10. **tend** (v.)

   a. _____

   b. _____ to be inclined; to move in a certain direction; to lead

Use the following list of synonyms and antonyms to fill in the blanks. Some words have no antonyms. In such cases, the antonym blanks have been marked with an X.

bring in	competing	don	isolation	observable	shed
business	cooperating	export	loaf	painstaking	toil
careless	destruction	incline	mingling	restoration	unnoticeable

	Synonyms	**Antonyms**
1. **imperceptible**	(unnoticeable)	(observable)
2. **scrupulous**	(painstaking)	(careless)
3. **renovation**	(restoration)	(destruction)
4. **lounge**	(loaf)	(toil)
5. **rival**	(competing)	(cooperating)
6. **establishment**	(business)	X
7. **import**	(bring in)	(export)
8. **tend**	(incline)	X
9. **quarantine**	(isolation)	(mingling)
10. **slough**	(shed)	(don)

Decide whether the first pair in the items below are synonyms or antonyms. Then choose the Master Word that shows a similar relation to the word(s) preceding the blank.

1. soar	:plunge	::neighborly	:	(rival)
2. delicate	:rugged	::ship abroad	:	(import)
3. surface	:bottom	::labor	:	(lounge)
4. principal	:secondary	::sloppy	:	(scrupulous)
5. tremble	:calm	::damage	:	(renovation)
6. phosphorescence	:shine	::aim	:	(tend)
7. harbor	:seaport	::separation	:	(quarantine)
8. congregate	:break up	::noticeable	:	(imperceptible)
9. concentration	:gathering	::peel	:	(slough)
10. swirl	:churning	::store	:	(establishment)

The Master Words in this lesson are repeated below. From the Master Words, choose the appropriate word for the blank in each of the following sentences. Write the word in the numbered space provided at the right.

| establishment | import | quarantine | rival | slough |
| imperceptible | lounge | renovation | scrupulous | tend |

1. Originally, to prevent the spread of diseases, a ...?... of forty days was required for the sick.

1. _____(quarantine)_____

2. A principal product ...?...(d, ed) from South America by the United States is coffee.

2. _____(import)_____

3. The ...?... teams enjoyed playing their yearly grudge match.

3. _____(rival)_____

4. During the ...?... of the downtown area, twelve old buildings were cleaned up and repaired.

4. _____(renovation)_____

5. Each time a rattlesnake ...?...(s) off old skin, it adds a new segment to its "rattle system."

5. _____(slough)_____

6. If the differences between "before" and "after" pictures are ...?..., the pictures surely have little point.

6. _____(imperceptible)_____

7. The chair was (a, an) ...?..., detailed reproduction of a fine antique.

7. _____(scrupulous)_____

8. Five business ...?...(s) were destroyed by the fire.

8. _____(establishment)_____

9. On summer afternoons Paul likes to ...?... beside the swimming pool, sleeping and reading.

9. _____(lounge)_____

10. Ron ...?...(s) to buy more expensive clothes than he can afford.

10. _____(tend)_____

To complete the crossword, choose the Master Word associated with each word or phrase below. Begin each answer in the square having the same number as the clue.

1. to ship in goods to sell

2. a needle in a haystack is this

3. project in some slum areas

4. many do this on the weekends

5. people with contagious diseases often endure this

6. thorough and precise

7. the other team

8. department store or restaurant

9. what you might do to dirty clothes or a bad habit

10. lean toward

Read the following selection to get the general meaning. Read it a second time, paying special attention to the words in dark type. Notice how they are used in sentences. These are Master Words. These are the words you will be working with in this lesson.

From **Walden**
by Henry David Thoreau

I did not read books the first summer; I hoed beans. Nay, I often did better than this. There were times when I could not afford to **sacrifice** the bloom of the present moment to any work, whether of the head or hands. I love a broad **margin** to my life. Sometimes, in a summer morning, having taken my accustomed bath, I sat in my sunny doorway from sunrise till noon, **rapt** in **reverie**, **amidst** the pines and hickories and sumacs, in **undisturbed** **solitude** and stillness, while the birds sang around or **flitted** noiseless through the house, until by the sun falling in at my west window, or the noise of some traveler's wagon on the distant highway, I was reminded of the **lapse** of time. I grew in those seasons like corn in the night, and they were far better than any work of the hands would have been. They were not time subtracted from my life, but so much over and above my usual **allowance.**

EXERCISE 1

SELF-TEST: After reading the above selection, do the following. Look at the Master Words below. Underline the words that you think you know. Circle the words that you are less sure about. Draw a square around the words you don't recognize.

MASTER WORDS

allowance	**rapt**
amidst	**reverie**
flit	**sacrifice**
lapse	**solitude**
margin	**undisturbed**

Read the selection on the preceding page again, this time paying special attention to the ten Master Words. In the (a) spaces provided below, write down what you think is the meaning of the word. After you have attempted a definition for each word, look up the word in a dictionary. In the (b) spaces, copy the appropriate dictionary definition.

1. **allowance** (n.)

    a. _____

    b. _____ regular portion or granted share _____

2. **amidst** (prep.)

    a. _____

    b. _____ in the middle of; among _____

3. **flit** (v.)

    a. _____

    b. _____ to flutter; to move lightly and quickly; to dart _____

4. **lapse** (n.)

    a. _____

    b. _____ a slipping or passing away, as of time _____

5. **margin** (n.)

    a. _____

    b. _____ a limit to what is possible or desirable _____

6. **rapt** (adj.)

    a. _____

    b. _____ completely absorbed or involved in _____

7. **reverie** (n.)

    a. _____

    b. _____ dreaminess; fanciful thoughts _____

8. **sacrifice** (v.)

    a. _____

    b. _____ to give up something desirable in order to gain something else, sometimes of even greater value _____

9. **solitude** (n.)

    a. _____

    b. _____ the state of being alone or apart from others ___

10. **undisturbed** (adj.)

    a. _____

    b. _____ without interference or interruption _____

Use the following list of synonyms and antonyms to fill in the blanks. Some words have no antonyms. In such cases, the antonym blanks have been marked with an X.

absorbed	companionship	disrupted	outside	portion	stagnation
aloneness	dart	forfeit	passage	reality	uninterested
among	daydream	gain	plod	scope	uninterrupted
boundlessness					

		Synonyms	**Antonyms**
1.	**sacrifice**	(forfeit)	(gain)
2.	**margin**	(scope)	(boundlessness)
3.	**rapt**	(absorbed)	(uninterested)
4.	**reverie**	(daydream)	(reality)
5.	**amidst**	(among)	(outside)
6.	**undisturbed**	(uninterrupted)	(disrupted)
7.	**solitude**	(aloneness)	(companionship)
8.	**flit**	(dart)	(plod)
9.	**lapse**	(passage)	(stagnation)
10.	**allowance**	(portion)	X

Decide whether the first pair in the items below are synonyms or antonyms. Then choose the Master Word that shows a similar relation to the word(s) preceding the blank.

1.	lounge	:idle	::border	: (margin)
2.	tend	:lean	::flutter	: (flit)
3.	rival	:supportive	::socializing	: (solitude)
4.	quarantine	:sequestering	::share	: (allowance)
5.	import	:ship overseas	::troubled	: (undisturbed)
6.	scrupulous	:reckless	::existence	: (reverie)
7.	slough	:remove	::give up	: (sacrifice)
8.	renovation	:decay	::outside	: (amidst)
9.	establishment	:shop	::period	: (lapse)
10.	imperceptible	:evident	::bored	: (rapt)

EXERCISE 5

The Master Words in this lesson are repeated below. From the Master Words, choose the appropriate word for the blank in each of the following sentences. Write the word in the numbered space provided at the right.

| allowance | flit | margin | reverie | solitude |
| amidst | lapse | rapt | sacrifice | undisturbed |

1. A beehive is one thing that is best left ...?... .

1. _____ (undisturbed)

2. Although the salesman continued to ...?... from one customer to another, he never seemed to make a sale.

2. _____ (flit)

3. Franklin realized that taking a part-time job would force him to ...?... some of the time he spent with his girlfriend.

3. _____ (sacrifice)

4. Rip Van Winkle had no idea that (a, an) ...?... of twenty years had occurred while he slept.

4. _____ (lapse)

5. Lucy felt small and unimportant as she stood ...?... the towering California redwoods.

5. _____ (amidst)

6. Michael is a loner who prefers ...?... even to the company of good friends.

6. _____ (solitude)

7. The ...?... for food makes up twenty percent of their budget.

7. _____ (allowance)

8. Aunt Helen was so ...?... in reading her book that she did not hear the knock on the door or the ring of the telephone.

8. _____ (rapt)

9. Bonnie tried to limit her immediate goals and narrow the ...?... of her possibilities.

9. _____ (margin)

10. People who spend much of their time in a ...?... tend to be impractical or creative geniuses.

10. _____ (reverie)

EXERCISE 6

The invented words below are formed from parts of different Master Words from this lesson. Create a definition and indicate the part of speech for each word. The first one is done for you.

sacrifilitude	*(n.) the act of sacrificing one's solitude*
allowerie	([n.] a dream about a big raise in your allowance)
marginflit	([v.] to dart from one extreme to another)
raptifice	([n.] a sacrifice made for the sake of a dearly loved person, hobby, etc.)

Now invent your own words by combining parts of the Master Words. Create a definition for each, and indicate the word's part of speech. (You may reuse any of the word parts above in new combinations.)

1. _____ _____

2. _____ _____

(Note: Answers will vary.)

Other possibilities:
raptflit	(v.) to become infatuated with one person after another
reverapt	(adj.) characterized by intense daydreaming
solifice	(v.) giving up one's peace and quiet

Read the following selection to get the general meaning. Read it a second time, paying special attention to the words in dark type. Notice how they are used in sentences. These are Master Words. These are the words you will be working with in this lesson.

From "The Lady, or the Tiger?"
by Frank R. Stockton

When her lover turned and looked at her, and his eye met hers as she sat there paler and whiter than anyone in the **vast** ocean of anxious faces about her, he saw, by that power of quick **perception** which is given to those whose souls are one, that she knew behind which door **crouched** the tiger, and behind which stood the lady. He had expected her to know it. He understood her nature, and his soul was **assured** that she would never rest until she had made plain to herself this thing, hidden to all other lookers-on, even to the king. The only hope for the youth in which there was any **element** of **certainty** was based upon the success of the princess in discovering this mystery; and the moment he looked upon her, he saw she had succeeded, as in his soul he knew she would succeed.

Then it was that his quick and anxious glance asked the question: "Which?" It was as plain to her as if he shouted it from where he stood. There was not an instant to be lost. The question was asked in a flash; it must be answered in another.

Her right arm lay on the cushioned **parapet** before her. She raised her hand, and made a slight, quick movement toward the right. No one but her lover saw her. Every eye but his was fixed on the man in the **arena**.

He turned, and with a firm and **rapid** step he walked across the empty space. Every heart stopped beating, every breath was held, every eye was fixed immovably upon that man. Without the slightest **hesitation**, he went to the door on the right and opened it.

Now, the point of the story is this: Did the tiger come out of that door, or did the lady?

EXERCISE 1

SELF-TEST: After reading the above selection, do the following. Look at the Master Words below. Underline the words that you think you know. Circle the words that you are less sure about. Draw a square around the words you don't recognize.

MASTER WORDS

arena	hesitation
assured	parapet
certainty	perception
crouch	rapid
element	vast

Read the selection on the preceding page again, this time paying special attention to the ten Master Words. In the (a) spaces provided below, write down what you think is the meaning of the word. After you have attempted a definition for each word, look up the word in a dictionary. In the (b) spaces, copy the appropriate dictionary definition.

1. **arena** (n.)

   a. _____

   b. _____ the area of an amphitheater where contests or performances are held; also, the scene of any competition

2. **assured** (adj.)

   a. _____

   b. _____ made sure; certain; confident

3. **certainty** (n.)

   a. _____

   b. _____ state of being certain or sure; confidence; beyond doubt

4. **crouch** (v.)

   a. _____

   b. _____ to stoop as if ready to spring, with the limbs close to the body

5. **element** (n.)

   a. _____

   b. _____ a part of a larger whole

6. **hesitation** (n.)

   a. _____

   b. _____ act of pausing, as if from uncertainty or indecision; a delay

7. **parapet** (n.)

   a. _____

   b. _____ a low wall or protective railing at the edge of a balcony, bridge, etc.

8. **perception** (n.)

   a. _____

   b. _____ ability to gain knowledge through observing with the senses; also, knowledge obtained in this way

9. **rapid** (adj.)

   a. _____

   b. _____ fast-moving; swift; quick

10. **vast** (adj.)

   a. _____

   b. _____ enormous; huge; large or wide

Use the following list of synonyms and antonyms to fill in the blanks. Some words have no antonyms. In such cases, the antonym blanks have been marked with an X.

awareness	doubtful	leisurely	quick	stretch	total
confident	huge	part	stadium	sureness	uncertainty
continuation	insensitivity	pause	stoop	tiny	wall

	Synonyms	**Antonyms**
1. **vast**	(huge)	(tiny)
2. **perception**	(awareness)	(insensitivity)
3. **crouch**	(stoop)	(stretch)
4. **assured**	(confident)	(doubtful)
5. **element**	(part)	(total)
6. **certainty**	(sureness)	(uncertainty)
7. **parapet**	(wall)	X
8. **arena**	(stadium)	X
9. **rapid**	(quick)	(leisurely)
10. **hesitation**	(pause) (uncertainty)	(continuation)(sureness)

Decide whether the first pair in the items below are synonyms or antonyms. Then choose the Master Word that shows a similar relation to the word(s) preceding the blank.

1. solitude	:company	::confused	:	(assured)
2. lapse	:passage	::delay	:	(hesitation)
3. margin	:range	::coliseum	:	(arena)
4. flit	:fly	::ingredient	:	(element)
5. reverie	:actuality	::slow	:	(rapid)
6. amidst	:apart	::question	:	(certainty)
7. rapt	:unconcerned	::small	:	(vast)
8. allowance	:amount	::squat	:	(crouch)
9. sacrifice	:surrender	::railing	:	(parapet)
10. undisturbed	:tranquil	::impression	:	(perception)

The Master Words in this lesson are repeated below. From the Master Words, choose the appropriate word for the blank in each of the following sentences. Write the word in the numbered space provided at the right.

| arena | certainty | element | parapet | rapid |
| assured | crouch | hesitation | perception | vast |

1. An optical illusion is an attempt to trick the powers of ...?... .

1. ___(perception)___

2. The sprinter ...?...(d, ed), his toe behind the chalk line, waiting for the starting gun to be fired.

2. ___(crouch)___

3. Melissa's ...?... and confident tone helped her win the debate.

3. ___(assured)___

4. Now we know with ...?... that a round trip between the earth and the moon is possible.

4. ___(certainty)___

5. The surprise ending is an important ...?... in a short story by O. Henry.

5. ___(element)___

6. Rival gangs fought for top position in the ...?... of the streets.

6. ___(arena)___

7. The crumbling ...?... was a hazard to people who crossed the bridge on foot.

7. ___(parapet)___

8. Some cities employ a ...?... transit system to move large numbers of people quickly during rush hour.

8. ___(rapid)___

9. The contestant's ...?... was natural when he was forced to decide between door number three or a cash prize.

9. ___(hesitation)___

10. The man who was used to shopping in a small store was confused by the ...?... selection of items in the supermarket.

10. ___(vast)___

Use at least five Master Words from this lesson to write a scene about one of the following topics. Or create a topic of your own. Write your choice on the blank. Circle the Master Words as you use them.

Possible Topics: The Last Two Minutes of the Game, A Visit to the Professor's Lab

_____

_____

_____

_____

_____

_____

_____

_____

(Note: Answers will vary.)

LESSON 36

PART I: From the list below, choose the appropriate word for each sentence that follows. Use each word only once. There will be two words left over.

allowance	concentration	margin	reservoir	undisturbed
appreciate	decent	parcel	retirement	wither
clatter	imperceptible	persuade	surface	

1. Some public figures claim that they would prefer _____ (retirement) _____ to being watched so closely by the press.

2. The P.O.W.s were granted (a, an) _____ (allowance) _____ of one bar of chocolate and one jar of coffee a month.

3. The smiling countenances of the senior citizens indicate how much they _____ (appreciate) _____ our Christmas concert.

4. During the dry spell, the city's _____ (reservoir) _____ reached its lowest level in twenty years.

5. Fresh paint covered up the graffiti and made the subway station look more _____ (decent) _____ .

6. _____ (Concentration) _____ of wealth among a few people tends to produce just two classes: the very rich and the very poor.

7. (A, An) _____ (parcel) _____ too large for the mailbox was left at the post office.

8. The snail moved so slowly that its progress was _____ (imperceptible) _____ .

9. The _____ (clatter) _____ of coins in his bank made Ron hopeful that he had finally saved enough to buy the model airplane.

10. Police officers were unable to _____ (persuade) _____ the suspect to surrender because the woman believed it was a trap.

11. Because Marie forgot to fill the vase with water, the flowers will quickly _____ (wither) _____ .

12. Todd desperately needed rest, so we let him sleep _____ (undisturbed) _____ on the couch.

PART II: Decide whether the first pair in the items below are synonyms or antonyms. Then choose a Master Word from Lessons 25-35 which shows a similar relation to the word(s) preceding the blank. Do not repeat a Master Word that appears in the first column.

1. wither   :flower   ::introduce   : _____ (cease)

2. check   :stop   ::enormous   : _____ (vast)

3. delicate   :brittle   ::broken down   : _____ (decrepit)

4. scrupulous :thorough   ::understanding : _____ (perception)

5. gloom   :grayness   ::heartlessness : _____ (brutality)

(Note: Other answers may be possible.)

PART III: From the list below, choose the appropriate word for each sentence that follows. Use each word only once. There will be two words left over.

afford	guise	renovation	snatch	squint
criticize	lounge	resigned	solitude	stature
discreet	probe	sacrifice	spacious	

1. Bob _____(snatch)_____(d, ed) the last sandwich before anyone else could grab it.

2. Many people who are quick to _____(criticize)_____ the establishment are slow in suggesting ways to improve it.

3. Scientists are beginning to _____(probe)_____ outer space to determine what kind of life may exist on other planets.

4. The _____(discreet)_____ burglar removed all evidence connecting him to the crime.

5. The farmers affirmed that their dry corn crop could not _____(afford)_____ another week without rain.

6. The _____(renovation)_____ of the older houses dressed up the entire neighborhood.

7. Though Barb offered the invitation under the _____(guise)_____ of friendship, Ian suspected she had other reasons for asking him to attend.

8. Some psychologists believe that Napoleon sought power in order to make up for his small _____(stature)_____.

9. With their team trailing 62-39 at the two-minute warning, most of the fans were _____(resigned)_____ to the fact that their team would lose.

10. Karen will _____(sacrifice)_____ her daily candy bar and send the money she saves to a fund for hungry children.

11. At first Cory enjoyed the _____(solitude)_____ of the big empty house, but he soon began to long for company.

12. After a week of hard work at math camp, we wanted to _____(lounge)_____ and relax.

PART IV: Decide whether the first pair in the items below are synonyms or antonyms. Then choose a Master Word from Lessons 25-35 which shows a similar relation to the word(s) preceding the blank. Do not repeat a master Word that appears in the first column.

1. modest	:gaudy	::uncertainly	:	(steadily)
2. quarantine	:mingling	::miss	:	(encounter)
3. merchant	:shopkeeper	::major	:	(principal)
4. import	:ship in	::gather	:	(congregate)
5. sort	:categorize	::hop	:	(flit)

(Note: Other answers may be possible.)

INDEX — Word and Lesson Number

A

abandon, 14
accommodating, 22
accustomed, 11
acknowledge, 21
adventurous, 5
affirm, 5
afford, 29
allowance, 34
ally, 23
amidst, 34
annoyance, 23
antics, 7
antiseptic, 3
anxious, 2
applicant, 8
appreciate, 27
arena, 35
aside, 3
assume, 7
assured, 35
attitude, 4

B

beseech, 15
blotchy, 1
blotter, 6
blustery, 15
bob, 31
bogged, 16
breeding, 2
brim, 10
brutality, 29

C

canter, 2
captivity, 19
cease, 31
certainty, 35
characterize, 20
charge, 11
check, 29
chuck, 15
chuckle, 6
chute, 18
clatter, 28

clench, 18
cloak, 17
coincidence, 6
collective, 11
compliment, 10
concentration, 32
congregate, 32
conjure, 19
conscientious, 11
conscious, 1
constant, 3
corrode, 28
councilor, 17
countenance, 23
crestfallen, 22
crisp, 27
criticize, 26
crouch, 35
crumple, 8
curious, 1
customary, 23

D

dampen, 13
dappled, 2
dart, 27
decent, 30
decrepit, 25
delicate, 32
deliverer, 19
dell, 30
deny, 4
depict, 14
descent, 18
despair, 8
desperate, 18
despondent, 2
destiny, 21
devise, 19
devour, 4
disabled, 2
discomfit, 26
discreet, 25
disengage, 5
disgust, 1
distribute, 3
drowse, 25

dun, 2
dunce, 14
duplication, 7
dusk, 28
dutiful, 8
dwindle, 22

E

economy, 22
elegant, 31
element, 35
employ, 5
enchantment, 19
encounter, 30
engaged, 15
entirely, 8
establishment, 33
excavate, 9
exclaim, 7
exhaustion, 15
existence, 21
expectation, 9
expert, 7
expression, 20

F

fakir, 1
fate, 1
fester, 29
fidgety, 2
filter, 10
flail, 18
flawless, 25
flicker, 25
flit, 34
flutter, 27
ford, 16
foresee, 23
fragile, 25
frank, 21
fretful, 4
frolic, 22

G

gambit, 6
garment, 26
garret, 27
gaze, 6
genie, 19
gilded, 17
glee, 11
glimpse, 18
gloom, 30
goad, 15
grate, 27
greedily, 4
guise, 25

H

harbor, 32
haunt, 30
haze, 9
hesitate, 3
hesitation, 35
humble, 13
humorous, 29
hunch, 9
hurtle, 18

I

immovable, 5
imperceptible, 33
implore, 19
import, 33
impractical, 17
impressive, 1
imprudent, 5
indefinite, 13
indicate, 26
individual, 11
inevitable, 23
inextricable, 31
inhabit, 21
injustice, 15
instinct, 16
intent, 4
interfere, 1
intersect, 7

ironical, 5
irregular, 9
irritate, 6

J

jar, 1
jumble, 31
junction, 7

K

knoll, 30

L

lapse, 34
latter, 13
lodge, 15
loophole, 20
lounge, 33
lurch, 9

M

maitre d', 8
manifest, 20
margin, 34
marvel, 7
mechanical, 3
meek, 20
merchant, 26
merciless, 16
mill, 16
misery, 29
mislead, 8
modest, 30
multicolored, 9
munch, 4
murmur, 3
mutter, 17

N

nape, 10
nobility, 20

O

oblige, 5
obstacle, 5
opalescent, 9
ordain, 21

P

painstaking, 26
parallel, 29
parapet, 35
parcel, 31
pattern, 7
pedestal, 17
peep, 11
perception, 35
personage, 13
perspiration, 28
persuade, 31
pert, 14
philosophy, 6
phosphorescence, 32
pitiful, 15
plight, 19
pluck, 27
plunge, 16
pomegranate, 27
porous, 10
portly, 14
posse, 7
pouch, 3
preserve, 13
presumptuous, 1
principal, 32
probe, 29
prop, 8
protrude, 14

Q

quarantine, 33

R

random, 10
rankle, 20
rapid, 35
rapt, 34
rapture, 11
rascal, 26
rave, 30
rebel, 19
recital, 21
refined, 25
reflective, 6
refresh, 4
regale, 22
relish, 3

rely, 5
remarkable, 2
render, 21
renovation, 33
reputation, 17
resentment, 20
reserve, 18
reservoir, 28
residence, 31
resigned, 26
resistance, 16
response, 29
restore, 21
retirement, 30
revelation, 22
reverie, 34
rival, 33
rubicund, 14

S

sacrifice, 34
sapphire, 17
scramble, 18
scrupulous, 33
select, 13
sensible, 17
sequestered, 30
serviceable, 14
severe, 17
shabby, 25
shrug, 6
shuffle, 2
single, 21
slash, 15
slough, 33
smirk, 26
smother, 11
snatch, 28
sneer, 26
soar, 32
society, 13
solitude, 34
sort, 28
spacious, 31
squall, 23
squint, 28
stately, 31
stature, 25
steadfast, 20
steadily, 29
strict, 22

submerge, 16
substantial, 13
surface, 32
suspect, 6
suspicion, 8
swirl, 32
swoop, 11
sympathetic, 13
sympathy, 3

T

tempestuous, 23
tend, 33
tidy, 22
tilt, 8
tingle, 9
tinkle, 9
trace, 22
tranquillity, 23
treacherous, 16
tremble, 32
trifle, 14
truncated, 28
tumbler, 27

U

undisturbed, 34
utter, 10

V

valet, 14
vast, 35
venture, 4
veranda, 10
vessel, 10
vigor, 20
vise, 10
vow, 19

W

wager, 23
weld, 28
wither, 27
wrangler, 16
wriggle, 4

Y

yowl, 18